GUIDEPOSTS

THE HIDDEN HAND OF GOD

AMAZING COINCIDENCES

THE HIDDEN HAND OF GOD

AMAZING COINCIDENCES

Surely there are in everyone's life certain connections, twists and
turns which pass awhile under the category of Chance, but at
the last, well examined, prove to be the very hand of God.
—Sir Thomas Browne

Guideposts®

CARMEL, NEW YORK 10512

www.guidepostsbooks.com

Acknowledgments

Every attempt has been made to credit the sources of copyrighted material used in this book. If any such acknowledgment has been inadvertently omitted or miscredited, receipt of such information would be appreciated.

All material that originally appeared in *Guideposts* magazine is reprinted with permission. Copyright © 1983, 1984, 1987, 1988, 1990, 1993 and 1997 by Guideposts, Carmel, New York 10512. All rights reserved.

All Scripture quotations, unless otherwise noted, are taken from *The Holy Bible, New International Version.* Copyright © 1973, 1978, 1984 International Bible Society. Used by permission of Zondervan Bible Publishers.

Scripture quotations marked (KJV) are taken from *The King James Version of the Bible.*

"A Baby Blanket" by Winona Smith appeared in *2nd Chicken Soup for the Woman's Soul* by Jack Canfield, Mark Victor Hansen, Jennifer Read Hawthorne, and Marci Shimoff. Copyright © 1998 by Winona Smith. Reprinted by permission of Winona Smith. Published by Health Communications, Inc.

"A Broken Taillight" from *Heaven Hears Each Whisper* by Kelsey Tyler. Copyright © 1996 by Karen Kingsbury. Used by permission of Putnam Berkley, A Division of Penguin Putnam Inc.

"A Coincidence?" by Ed Koper appeared in *Chicken Soup for the Christian Soul* by Jack Canfield, Mark Victor Hansen, Patty Aubery, and Nancy Mitchell. Copyright © 1997 by Ed Koper. Reprinted by permission of Ed Koper. Published by Health Communications, Inc.

"A Sweater Comes Home" by Becky Alexander, "The Christmas Eve Gift" by Mary Welker and "Cold Call" reprinted with permission from *Small Miracles of Love and Friendship* by Judith Leventhal and Yitta Halberstam © 1999. Published by Adams Media Corporation.

"A Textbook Example" by Roberta Messner appeared in *Mother's Miracles*, compiled and edited by Jamie C. Miller, Laura Lewis, and Jennifer Basye Sander. Copyright © 1999 by Jamie C. Miller, Laura Lewis, and Jennifer Basye Sander. Published by William Morrow and Company, Inc.

"About Twenty-Five Cents" by Cathe Odom appeared in *Heavenly Miracles*, compiled and edited by Jamie C. Miller, Laura Lewis, and Jennifer Basye Sander. Copyright © 2000 by Jamie C. Miller, Laura Lewis, and Jennifer Basye Sander. Published by William Morrow and Company, Inc.

(continued on pages 174 and 175)

THE HIDDEN HAND OF GOD
AMAZING COINCIDENCES

If a man does not believe that all the world is God's family, where nothing happens by chance but is all guided and directed by the care and providence of a being that is all love and goodness to all of his creatures; if a man does not believe this from his heart, he cannot truly be said to believe in God.
—*William Law*

Chance. Accident. Luck. Happenstance. Coincidence.

How often do we credit the blessings of our lives to the random forces of the universe, rather than to the hand of a loving God? Coincidence is the word that we often use when we try to describe events that occur with inexplicable timing. According to Merriam Webster, a coincidence is "the occurrence of events that happen at the same time by accident but seem to have some connection."

Of course, those who understand God to have His hand on our lives recognize that there is really no such thing as accident or coincidence. What seems inexplicable or accidental is simply God's perfect timing.

Remember the story of Esther, her cousin Mordecai, and Haman, the wicked enemy of the Jews? Born in Persia as part of the exiled Jewish community, Esther was a beautiful young Jewish woman who basically won a beauty contest to become the queen of King Xerxes. The ever-faithful Mordecai overheard a plot to kill the king; he warned Esther, who in turn warned Xerxes, thus saving the life of the king. But Mordecai became embroiled in a nasty feud with Haman, a special favorite of the king. Haman was furious that Mordecai wouldn't give him the respect he thought he deserved. He determined to kill Mordecai, and not just Mordecai, but all of the Jews throughout the entire kingdom. Haman convinced King Xerxes to allow him to send troops throughout the kingdom to kill "all these people who didn't obey the king's laws." Xerxes agreed, signed the degree, and couriers were dispatched to carry the irrevocable death sentence to all the king's provinces.

Esther learned of this situation when Mordecai sent her a message, explaining Haman's plot and Xerxes' decree, begging her to intervene with the king. When she reminded him that she could be put to death if she dared approach the king without an invitation, Mordecai did not mince words: "Do not think that because you are in the king's house you alone of all the Jews will escape. For if you remain silent at this time, relief and deliverance for the Jews will arise from another place, but you and your father's family will perish. And who knows but that you have come to royal position for such a time as this?"

After three days of fasting and preparation, Esther approached the king, who agreed to grant her petition. She then invited the king and Haman to attend a special feast she would prepare for them. Haman left the palace, elated to be the queen's guest of honor, but his joy soured when, at the gate, he passed Mordecai, who still refused to bow down to him. Haman went home to boast to his friends and family about finding great favor with the queen and to complain bitterly about his nemesis Mordecai. They advised him to build a seventy-five-foot gallows on which he could hang Mordecai first thing in the morning and then go enjoy his feast with the king and queen. So Haman built the gallows.

Meanwhile, back at the palace, the king was having difficulty sleeping. He called for his aides to read to him from the record books that chronicled his reign. Included in these records was the story of Mordecai's warning—which had saved the king's life. King Xerxes realized nothing had ever been done to honor Mordecai for this great deed, and he purposed in his mind to reward him.

Later that day, at Esther's banquet, King Xerxes asked her again to reveal her petition. And Esther stopped the show: "If I have found favor with you, O king, and if it pleases your majesty, grant me my life—this is my petition. And spare my people—this is my request. For I and my people have been sold for destruction and slaughter and annihilation." The king was horrified and demanded, "Who did this?" And Esther told him: "Haman." Well, she really said, "The adversary and enemy is this vile Haman."

Haman is hung on the gallows he built for Mordecai. Mordecai is given the king's ring and made a royal official. And Xerxes issues an order to counteract the death decree, giving Jews throughout Persia the right to assemble and to protect themselves.

The story of Esther turns on a series of extraordinary coincidences: Esther just "happened" to be selected as King Xerxes' new queen. The king just "happened" to be unable to sleep, and then he just "happened" across the account of Mordecai's valor. These coincidences, coupled with Esther's courage, shifted this story from one of tragedy for the Jews to one of victory.

So, were these really mere coincidences? God is never mentioned in the book of Esther and indeed, sometimes seems deliberately left out. But for readers who believe, there is no doubt of God's handiwork. All of life is under God's command.

In this book are stories of amazing coincidences, miracles in the ordinary and the every day. These stories reassure us that, whatever the circumstances, God's own hand is on our lives.

"For my thoughts are not your thoughts,

neither are your ways my ways,"

declares the LORD.

"As the heavens are higher than the earth,

so are my ways higher than your ways

and my thoughts than your thoughts."

—Isaiah 55:8–9

Chapter 1   Perfect Timing

To most of us "perfect timing" means being in the right place at the right time; we find a special deal, meet someone, avoid a mishap. Perhaps perfect timing is having every dish you're serving at a dinner party done at the same time, or getting to the post office two seconds before they close the door.

But are we crediting chance for what God is doing? We lucked out; our stars were in confluence; fortune was smiling on us. And even if we don't use these same words, we silently subscribe to their meaning: It's merely chance, accident, good timing, coincidence. Of course, intellectually we know that God does not involve luck; His plan is not about chance or happenstance.

God guides our steps carefully. What we call coincidence is, in truth, God's timing. We find ourselves taking a different route home only to find out later that we missed a serious multicar collision. We shop at a different grocery store and run into someone we lost track of years before. We receive a check just in time to meet a special obligation.

The universe, our worlds and all of these scenarios have been set in motion by a loving God, Who continues to guide and direct our lives according to His perfect timing.

O LORD, you have searched me

and you know me.

You know when I sit and when I rise;

you perceive my thoughts from afar.

You discern my going out and my lying down;

you are familiar with all my ways.

Before a word is on my tongue

You know it completely, O LORD.

You hem me in—behind and before;

you have laid your hand upon me.

Such knowledge is too wonderful for me,

too lofty for me to attain.

—Psalm 139:1–6

COLD CALL

YITTA HALBERSTAM AND JUDITH LEVENTHAL

From childhood on, Nathan Stein always dreamed about becoming a doctor, but it was a dream he had first to defer and then, ultimately to abandon.

Only one year into college, the Depression imposed its stark reality upon his family, as it did upon countless other millions. Forced to quit school and get a job to help support his parents and siblings, Nathan saw his dreams slowly dwindle away. *Maybe one day a child of mine, or at least a child of theirs will be able to become the doctor I never could be*, he sighed.

Decades later, Nathan began to pin his hopes on his grandson, Kevin Landin, with whom he had an especially warm relationship. "Kevin," he used to repeat over and over again, "I hope you'll become the doctor I always wanted to be." Sadly, when Kevin was only nine years old, Nathan Stein died. But the dreams he had so passionately implanted in Kevin lived on.

For Kevin, like his grandfather, had committed himself at a young age to pursuing the goal Nathan Stein had never been able to achieve in his own lifetime. He wanted to become a physician and heal the sick. And, as time passed, the dream became more entrenched in his mind, being, and soul.

But where to find the money for medical school? When Kevin, twenty-three, was a senior at Pennsylvania State University, he began to apply to various medical schools with a high level of anxiety. How would he pay the first year's medical tuition of fifteen thousand dollars? His parents both worked as real estate brokers, and they stepped up their efforts to bring in more business.

One day, his father, Sherman Ladin, noticed an ad in a local paper placed by an owner trying to sell his own residence.

"Normally, I don't call people who advertise on their own," Sherman Ladin told *The Philadelphia Inquirer*. But, as he explained to the newspaper, he was suddenly seized by an uncontrollable urge to call the number, an urge he couldn't quite explain. It was uncharacteristic of him to pursue business in this manner.

The owners weren't very receptive to his "cold" call, either. They wanted to sell the house themselves and forego a broker's commission. They told Sherman they would wait several days to see what kind of response they got to their ad. If they couldn't sell the house on their own, they'd eventually call him back—they promised.

And they did.

The owners arranged for Sherman to come see the house on a Tuesday. The appointment was formally set and Sherman penciled it into his calendar. But when he told his wife, she exclaimed with surprise: "What? Did you forget we're going to Atlantic City on Tuesday? You have to change that appointment!"

Sherman called the homeowners and a new appointment was rescheduled for Monday afternoon at 3:00 P.M. "Three o'clock it is then!" he confirmed. But later that day, the homeowners called *him* and said that now *they* had to change the time. The third—and final—appointment was scheduled for Monday morning at 11:00 A.M.

When Sherman approached the house, whose address he had been given, he experienced a minor shock. "When I walked up to the front door, I realized that this was the same house my in-laws had lived in fifteen years before, and it was a very strange feeling," he recalled.

As Sidney and Dina Toporov, current owners of the house, ushered him into the living room, he began to tell them about the strange coincidence. But he barely had a chance to say a few words when the doorbell rang.

"No, I'm sorry, but there's some mistake," he heard the Toporovs tell the mail carrier at the door who was holding a certified letter in his hand. "There's no one here by that name. We never heard of a Nathan Stein. . . ."

Shermain Ladin jumped up from his chair. "That was my father-in-law!" he exclaimed.

Telling the mail carrier that his father-in-law was dead fourteen years, he offered to sign for the registered letter, which just happened to be from a bank.

It was a notice about a dormant account that had never been claimed. A dormant account of Nathan Stein's that no one—not his wife nor his daughter nor his son-in-law —knew anything about. An account that would be forfeited to the state if it would not be claimed soon. An account that contained fifteen thousand dollars!

"I am sure my father wanted my husband to be in his old house at the exact time that the mailman came with the registered letter," Shirley Ladin, Nathan's daughter, told reporters. "It had to be that way. Can you think of any other reason for that happening?"

Her husband agreed.

"I was put in that house at precisely that time to make sure Kevin would get the money for his first year's medical tuition," Sherman Ladin said.

"My father was always there to make things right for us, and he's still doing it," Shirley Ladin said. "There's no doubt in my mind that my father made this happen and that he's watching us to this day."

THE CHECK IS IN THE MAIL

ELIZABETH MULLOY

A few years ago when my parents passed away, I, an only child, found myself with what was, to my eyes, a sizable inheritance. My parents had always tithed, so my husband and I felt led to send a tenth of the money to a missionary among the poorest of Oklahoma's Native Americans. Being from Texas, I had seen for myself the poverty and despair of people on the reservations, and I deeply admired this faithful woman who had chosen to spend her long life showing them God's love.

In addition, I'd heard that she had recently broken a hip, so I concluded that the gift would be God's way of covering some of her medical bills. But because of the size of the gift I procrastinated, wanting to be "sure" the money would be useful. When I finally telephoned her to find out how to make out the check, I learned that an international women's group had already paid all of her hospital expenses!

Days, weeks, even months passed as I questioned the Lord: Are You sure You want me to send her the full amount? A mysterious Scripture floated to mind: the story of Mary, pouring out her ointment upon Jesus as He said, "She has kept this for my burial."

Unable to make sense of it, I finally got the check into the mail just as our family was leaving for our annual vacation at the beach. I realized to my dismay that it had been something like six months since the Lord had first told me to send it. The need had long ago been answered, I thought, apologizing to the Lord and resolving to be quicker to obey next time.

When we returned home and looked through our mail, an Oklahoma postmark jolted my memory. As our missionary friend graciously thanked us, she gave testimony to God's goodness; in the process of erecting the first church they'd ever had, her little congregation had been stalled by the cost of the next phase of building. Months had passed, and people were losing hope of ever having a special place in which to worship God. My friend had struggled with what to do. The only money she had ever saved for her own purposes was for her funeral expenses: a widow with no family for more than forty years, she had never wanted to burden "her" Indians, even by her death. But the Lord seemed to be pointing to this sum as the answer to the church project. It would be the ultimate sacrificial gift of her life, but she gave it quickly, figuring "the Lord could always just take me away, like Elijah!"

But God had other plans. In the next day's mail had come our check—for the exact amount she had just relinquished to God's call. The church project could continue and her precious "ointment"—kept for a burial, to be sure—had been replenished by One Who sees and orchestrates all things for good.

When I called her with my side of the story, we both praised God for His sovereignty and mercy.

Psalm 139 tells us that God knows our thoughts "from afar off"; I saw that God knew what needed to be in the mail on that July day. He also knew that if He used me, He'd have to start the ball rolling in January! How glad I am that He never gave up.

THE MIRACLE ON SHERBROOKE STREET

STEPHEN LAUDI

Montreal used to be known as "The City of Churches." The role of the church in the city has declined somewhat over the years, but the influence can still be seen in the way that all of Montreal embraces the Christmas season. The efforts of residents, merchants and city workers alike turn the city's wide boulevards into a glittering fantasyland ablaze with decorations and lights. And it was on one of those wide boulevards that our Christmas miracle occurred.

I was the president of the community council for Notre Dame de Grace that year. One of my duties involved organizing a big public caroling party. We wanted to involve not just church members, but as many people from the surrounding community as we could. Christmas is a wonderful time of year to reach out, and we hoped that our party, "A Christmas Caroling," would accomplish that. We invited many choir members (and anyone else who could carry a tune) and friends to join us one night on the sidewalk of Sherbrooke Street.

Sherbrooke Street is a wide downtown street lined with stately old elm trees. The heavy branches of the trees were gaily decorated with colored Christmas lights, which were reflected in turn on the dark, slick streets below. It was a magical look. The turnout was great, a group of thirty-five adults and children all bundled up against the snowy night, clutching songbooks in their gloved hands. A multitude of voices soon filled the air as we warmed up with a few of the old Yuletide favorites: "Hark the Herald Angels Sing" and "The Twelve Days of Christmas." I was excited; this community event was everything I'd hoped for, with one small exception. It was *cold*.

Our plan was to stand on the sidewalk and sing for passersby instead of going door-to-door. As we assembled to begin, I noticed a few singers look longingly into the frosted windows of a restaurant behind us. The restaurant was pleased at the presence of such a large group of singers and had even offered to give us all free hot chocolate that evening. I decided that the time for hot chocolate had arrived.

The group of singers filed one by one down the eight narrow stairs that led into the small restaurant, grateful that a warm drink was on its way. We stood together in the center of the room, waiting for our group to reassemble at the tables. A small parade came slowly down the stairs. It took a few minutes before the last of our group stepped into the restaurant. And then it happened.

No sooner did we all sit down than a loud crash rang out. The underground building shook, and we rushed up the stairs toward the door. And there, at the very spot on the sidewalk where our large group of singers had stood just moments before, lay a large electrical truck, its broken wheels spinning. The driver of the Hydro-Quebec truck had lost control on a patch of black ice as he drove down Sherbrooke Street and crashed head-on into the street lamp.

We did sing our carols that night. Too shaken to stand out on the street again, we stayed down in the restaurant and sang for the truck driver, the police, and the owners of the restaurant whose generous offer of a cup of hot chocolate had spared us all.

SOLDIER TO THE RESCUE

JOAN WESTER ANDERSON

Steve Campbell still cannot explain why he made a decision that could have ended in dangerous consequences. "You do what you have to do," he says simply.

Steve, a soldier stationed at Fort Bragg, North Carolina, was preparing to take his three children on a six hundred and fifty-mile drive to his parents' house for Thanksgiving. Unfortunately, his wife couldn't come because she had to work. "During the time we've lived at Fort Bragg, I've made the trip to my folk's house in Radcliff, Kentucky, several times, both day and night," Steve says. So he knows the roads well and wasn't concerned about driving as night turned into Thanksgiving morning.

But this time he had taken the family van, which uses gas more quickly than his other car. "I noticed on the outskirts of Lexington, Kentucky, about 2:30 A.M., that I was getting low and ought to stop for gas," Steve says. "But the last open station I passed in Lexington was on the other side of the highway, with a median between us, and I didn't want to stop and turn around." He'd be heading onto the Bluegrass Parkway, he knew, and there would be one open oasis after another. He'd watch for the next one.

But to Steve's mounting concern, each rest area that he passed was closed and darkened. He belatedly realized that because it was a holiday, nothing would be open. This was a bad situation. There was no way he was going to get to his parents' house now, his gauge had been on E for some time already. It was unusually cold that night, and although the children were snug under the few blankets he'd brought along, what would happen if the car ran out of gas and the heater went off? He hadn't seen another car in miles, and he knew this stretch of highway had few if any houses on it. And when the van eventually ran out of gas—well, Steve was a big man and a tough GI. But would he be able to protect all three of his children if they were set upon by criminals?

Although sputtering, the van continued to travel. Oddly, it had gone more than 100 miles since Lexington, Steve realized; he wouldn't have thought he could have gotten that far. And then his luck finally ran out. The engine died, and the van coasted to a stop on a desolate stretch of road, with no highway lights to show them where they were and no drivers with cell phones to flag down.

Steve switched off the headlights and opened the door. Might as well see where he was, he said to himself. Maybe there was a house nearby.

It was then that he heard it. A woman's voice, calling weakly. "Help. Help me."

It must be his imagination, he thought. Who would be out here at four-thirty in the morning?

"Help." The plea came again. It sounded like it was somewhere below him.

Thoughts flooded his mind. It could be someone in distress . . . or a trap, with thugs waiting for him to go down a pitch-dark embankment so they could ambush and mug him. How could he leave the kids alone in the car while he went to investigate? But how could he walk away from someone who might be hurt or even dying?

He made his decision quickly, taking several road flares and setting them up behind his van to protect it. He grabbed a flashlight. "Watch my light," he told his oldest son. "If it goes out, you'll know I've been mugged. Then turn the flares off and lock the van doors." Steve went to the edge of the road and sent the thin stream of light downward. There, in a ditch about twenty feet below, was a crumpled car. "It could barely be seen unless you were standing right over it," he says. "A casual passerby would not have ever noticed it."

"Help me," the voice cried again. It was coming from the car.

Swiftly Steve scrambled down the bluff. The car was overturned and coated with ice—it looked, he thought, as if it had been abandoned there for months. Yet he had heard that voice. He peered inside the wreckage, but no one was there. "Hello?" he called. "Where are you?"

"Here," came the voice. Steve circled the car and finally found a young woman lying on her side in the frozen mud, her hips and legs pinned under the car. She had been trapped there, she whispered, since she'd lost control of her car and it went over the side of the ditch, about eight hours earlier. No one had heard her cries. The temperature was now twenty-five degrees.

Steve took a few moments to reassure her. "I think I better not try and move you—I might do more harm than good," he said. But when he heard the sound of a truck rumbling down the highway, he ran back up the hill and flagged it down with his flashlight. While the trucker called for help on his CB radio, Steve grabbed his jack and the blankets, clambered back down the embankment, used the jack to lift the car off the victim, and kept her as warm as possible. Within thirty minutes the woman was being loaded into a rescue helicopter. Steve learned later that she had suffered several broken bones but would recover.

One of the officials at the scene saw to it that Steve got some gas, and the Campbells continued on their way. "I honestly didn't think anything more about it," Steve says, "until later that day. My mother thanked God at our Thanksgiving meal for bringing me there at the right time to help that lady." Then Steve started to think a little harder. Given the fact that the distance between his parents' house and his is six hundred and fifty miles, and given the fact that the van seemed to travel longer than usual on E, what were the odds that Steve would run out of gas at the exact spot where a young woman was in desperate need of help?

"Maybe that lady's guardian angel took care of it all," Steve muses. But not without an earthly angel who was asked to accept a mission—and said yes.

MIRACLE AT THE NATIONAL ARCHIVES

Jan Noble

Have you ever wondered if God knew about you, *really* cared about you, and was concerned about what happened to you? I suppose my husband Rich was not so different from most people when he began to ask that question. Adoptees especially can have feelings of rejection, stemming from unanswered questions about their birth parents. But for Rich, these feelings were further compounded by an adoptive mother who abandoned him to be raised by his adoptive father's mother.

To all outward appearances, Rich had everything he had ever wanted in life: a wife, a family of his own and a good job as a budget analyst at the Pentagon that enabled him to support them. However, when Rich reached midlife, a profound longing to know his father's identity began to surface. "Honey, should we start searching for your birth family?" I would ask, to which Rich always replied, "If they didn't want me, I don't want them." But deep down, at the very core of his being, there were questions surrounding his birth that haunted him. *Why didn't my mother keep me? Didn't she want me? Did my father even know I existed? Did he care? Didn't he want me either? Why didn't anyone come looking for me?*

When I saw Rich weeping as he viewed the latest TV show on a father-son relationship, I decided I would start searching for his family. During the two-year search we learned that while Rich's adoption papers listed his name as George Robert Casselman, his birth certificate listed his name as "Baby Boy Hicks." But more disappointing, the space for father's name had been left blank. The search for Rich's father would require more imagination and determination than most adoption searches, eventually leading me to the National Archives in Washington, D.C.

The echo of my footsteps on the marble floor of the National Archives was a persistent reminder that I was a woman on a mission. The clock above the sign-in desk outside the microfilm research room read 12:30 P.M. It was later than I had hoped to arrive, but I knew the research room stayed open until 9:00 P.M. on Tuesdays. Rich would be working late, so I had all the time I needed to search through the census records for his birth mother's family.

Census records are stored on microfilm at the National Archives and as I signed the register, the efficient woman stationed at the sign-in desk was already handing me a paper with the number of the microfilm reader to which I was assigned. Stepping across the threshold into this carpeted cavernous room, I realized reader number ninety-six would be in the last row at the opposite end of the room.

Walking towards my assigned reader, I thought *Has this search for Rich's family really been going on for two years? It seems agonizingly slow and I have so little hope of discovering his father's identity. Lord, only You can help me. Give me the wisdom for whatever the next step is in this process.*

My first shock was discovering that the latest census information available is from 1920, since an Act of Congress prohibits census information from being released for seventy-two years. That meant that I couldn't start with census records from the time of Rich's birth, so I had to determine what sort of information I could glean from the records of 1900, 1910, and 1920, the years that would cover his mother's life.

I started searching the census reel for 1900 for Waupaca, Wisconsin, which was listed as his mother's birthplace on Rich's original birth certificate. Waupaca, a county or a town? I didn't know. All I did know was that his mother's maiden name was Ruth Hicks and her married name was Casselman. Although Ruth was born in 1902, I began by searching for her family's listing under the name of Hicks in the 1900 census reel.

A few hours later, I was walking towards the Copy Room with some of my findings and overheard a man mention Wisconsin. He was seated next to a woman using the Enlarged Reader (available for the visually impaired). These specialized readers are in the first row of this very large room and my reader was in the last row, at the opposite end of the room.

On the way back to my reader, I stopped at the file drawers to pick up the 1920 census reel. Not finding the Hicks' family listing, I checked for a separate listing for Ruth since she would be eighteen by then and possibly living on her own. Bingo . . . there she was.

Encouraged to find that she was still in Wisconsin in 1920, I trudged back to the file drawer again, this time for the 1910 census reel. It was missing! "Excuse me. Is there another location where the 1910 census reel for Waupaca, Wisconsin might be filed?" I asked the librarian. "No," she assured me, "it's in that drawer. Someone has probably misfiled it." I searched that drawer and the next . . . no Waupaca, Wisconsin. I couldn't believe it. Even at the National Archives, the Waupaca census reel wouldn't exactly be on the bestseller list.

Remembering the couple at the front of the room and the overheard reference to Wisconsin, I decided to just casually saunter behind them and see what reel they had displayed on their screen. I looked at the screen and there it was—Waupaca County, Wisconsin. Amazed, I said to the man, "Pardon me, but you have the census reel I've been looking for."

"Really? Who are you looking for?"

I responded, "Ruth Hicks." The woman gasped and pointed to the bottom of her screen. She had just pulled Ruth Hicks' name up on the bottom line of the screen. I couldn't believe it! I said, "Well, really, I'm looking for the children of Ruth Hicks . . ." and she completed my sentence, ". . . Casselman!" I was just stunned. The man looked at her and extended his arm towards her in one of those "ta dah!" gestures. The woman smiled, "She was my mother."

By then, my mind was just whirring, trying to comprehend what was happening. I was still looking at this woman trying to understand if she was actually a sister of Rich's when the man said, "We're looking for the baby brother." I looked at the man and stammered, "I married the baby brother. He's working at the Pentagon two stops down on the Metro line."

The woman introduced herself as Shirley Casselman Garnett. The man with her, a member of the family who is a genealogist, was showing her how to do microfilm research in an attempt to find her baby brother.

"What is my brother's name?" Shirley asked.

"Rich Noble."

"His name isn't George? I remember my mother saying she'd named him George." "Yes," I replied, "that was the name given on the adoption papers: George Robert Casselman."

Her relative said, "Well, his real father's name was Thomas Miller, so I've been looking for a George Miller for twenty years." With a quavering voice, Shirley said,

"I was the last member of my family to hold my baby brother. I was only six, but I've dreamed all my life of someday meeting my brother. I needed to know that he was all right and hoped he had a happier life than I had."

Shirley went on to fill in the gaps left unanswered by official records; Rich's father was not Ruth Casselman's husband, and Rich's birth precipitated the divorce of Shirley's parents. All their children had subsequently been raised in orphanages. And although Rich's father wanted him, and had fought to keep him, Ruth had instead given him up for adoption.

With shaking hands, I dialed Rich's number at work. When he answered, he sounded awful.

"What's wrong, honey?"

He told me he had received a voice mail message around 10:30 that morning saying that his adoptive mother had died. Although she hadn't actually raised him, it was still a shock.

I asked, "Honey, are you sitting down?" When he said he was, I continued, "I'm at the National Archives, and I just met your sister." I could hear Rich's voice catch and then heard his sobbing over the phone as he realized that not only had the Lord miraculously allowed me to meet his only living sibling but also the one person who had been longing to find him all these years.

"Honey, there's more—they know who your father was. His name was Thomas Miller. Not only did he know you existed, honey, but he wanted to keep you."

We arranged to meet Rich at the Pentagon and then go to dinner to have some time to get acquainted. As we visited during dinner, the Lord's hand and orchestration of the smallest details became apparent in the miraculous reunion that we were experiencing. No person can take credit for our meeting. No genealogy research could have brought us together. No genealogist, no matter how skilled, could have followed a paper trail that would lead to a George Miller. My husband never existed as George Miller.

If Shirley and her relative had already used the 1910 Waupaca census reel and returned it to the file drawer, I would never have met them. And it was only because Shirley was using an Enlarged Reader at the front of the room that I was able to observe what microfilm she had projected onto the screen.

Shirley had flown in from Hawaii to see her son who was a patient at one of the local medical centers, and was scheduled to fly home the next morning (on her birthday). She told us that the only thing she had wanted for her birthday was to know that her baby brother was all right and that he grew up knowing he was loved (something Shirley herself did not experience). Shirley was a heart patient and required permission from her doctor to fly in to see her son. Little did she know that the Lord would graciously give her the desire of her heart on this trip.

My husband is now at peace since he finally has the truth regarding the circumstances of his birth. Growing up, Rich often felt unloved, rejected and abandoned by all the adults in his life. Now he can see the Lord's protection and provision for him by sparing him from dreadful home situations. This has been a powerful lesson in learning to give thanks in everything and then watching the good that the Lord can work out in our lives in even the most difficult circumstances.

GOD CALLING

JOAN WESTER ANDERSON

It had always been Ken Gaub's goal to help those who were hurting. "Some people just need a little boost, and I wanted to influence their lives in a positive way," he says. He became a traveling missionary and, with his family, conducted crusades not only throughout America but in many foreign countries. He established a magazine, a radio and television ministry, and a youth outreach program.

But sometimes even preachers get drained and discouraged, and they wonder if they should consider another line of work. That was how Ken felt one day in the 1970s as he, his wife Barbara, and their children drove their two ministry buses down I-75 just south of Dayton, Ohio. *God, am I doing any good, traveling around like this, telling people about You?* he wondered silently. *Is this what You want me to do?*

"Hey, Dad, let's get some pizza!" one of Ken's sons suggested. Still lost in thought, Ken turned off at the next exit, Route 741, where one sign after another advertised a wide variety of fast food. *A sign*, Ken mused. *That's what I need, God, a sign.*

Ken's son and daughter-in-law had already maneuvered the second bus into a pizza parlor's parking lot, and they stood waiting as Ken pulled up. The rest of the family bounced down the steps. Ken sat staring into space.

"Coming?" Barbara asked.

"I'm not really hungry," Ken told her. "I'll stay out here and stretch my legs."

Barbara followed the others into the restaurant, and Ken stepped outside, closed the bus doors, and looked around. Noticing a Dairy Queen, he strolled over, bought a soft drink, and ambled back still pondering. He was exhausted. But were his doldrums a sign of permanent burnout?

A persistent ringing broke Ken's concentration. The jangle was coming from a pay telephone in a booth at the service station right next to the Dairy Queen. As Ken approached the booth, he looked to see if anyone in the station was coming to answer the phone. But the attendant continued his work, seemingly oblivious to the noise.

Why didn't someone answer it? Ken wondered, growing irritated. What if it was an emergency?

The insistent ringing went on. Ten rings. Fifteen . . .

Curiosity overcame Ken's lethargy. Walking to the booth, he lifted the receiver. "Hello?"

"Long-distance call for Ken Gaub," came the voice of the operator.

Ken was stunned. "You're crazy!" he said. Then, realizing his rudeness, he tried to explain. "This can't be! I was just walking down the road here, and the phone was ringing. . . ."

The operator ignored his ramblings. "Is Ken Gaub there?" she asked. "I have a long-distance call for him."

Was this a joke? Automatically, Ken smoothed his hair for the "Candid Camera" crew that must surely appear. But no one came. His family was eating pizza in a randomly selected restaurant just a few yards from where he stood. And no one else knew he was here.

"I have a long-distance call for Ken Gaub, sir," the operator said again, obviously reaching the limits of her patience. "Is he there or isn't he?"

"Operator, I'm Ken Gaub," Ken said, still unable to make sense of it.

"Are you sure?" the operator asked, but just then, Ken heard another woman's voice on the telephone.

"Yes, that's him, Operator!" she said. "Mr. Gaub, I'm Millie from Harrisburg, Pennsylvania. You don't know me, but I'm desperate. Please help me."

"What can I do for you?" Ken asked. The operator hung up.

Millie began to weep, and Ken waited patiently for her to regain control. Finally she explained: "I was about to kill myself, and I started to write a suicide note. Then I began to pray and tell God I really didn't want to do this." Through her desolation, Millie remembered seeing Ken on television. If she could just talk to that nice, kindly minister, the one with the understanding attitude. . . .

"I knew it was impossible because I didn't know how to reach you," Millie went on, calmer now. "So I started to finish the note. And then some numbers came into my mind, and I wrote them down." She began to weep again. Silently Ken prayed for the wisdom to help her.

"I looked at those numbers," Millie continued tearfully, "and I thought—wouldn't it be wonderful if I had a miracle from God, and He has given me Ken's phone number? I can't believe I'm talking to you. Are you in your office in California?"

"I don't have an office in California," Ken explained. "It's in Yakima, Washington."

"Then where are you?" Millie asked, puzzled.

Ken was even more bewildered. "Millie, don't you know? You made the call."

"But I don't know what area this is." Millie had dialed the long-distance operator and given the numbers to her, making it a person-to-person call. And somehow she had found Ken in a parking lot in Dayton, Ohio.

Ken gently counseled the woman. Soon she met the One who would lead her out of her situation into a new life. Then he hung up the phone, still dazed. Would his family believe this incredible story? Perhaps he shouldn't tell anyone about it.

But he had prayed for an answer, and he had received just what he needed—a renewed sense of purpose, a glimpse of the value of his work, an electrifying aware-ness of God's concern for each of His children—all in an encounter that could only have been arranged by His heavenly Father.

Ken's heart overflowed with joy. "Barb," he explained as his wife climbed back into the bus. "You won't believe this! God knows where I am!"

Chapter 2 Crossing Paths

None of us are here by accident. We each fit into a bigger plan, a plan created by God, which unfolds according to His timing. And each of us has a special purpose. So it shouldn't surprise us when people come into our lives who—coincidently—are key contributors to completing the tasks we've been given.

We all get caught up in our lives, focusing intently on our work, our families, our own goals and achievements. We consider ourselves successful and happy. Then someone slips into our lives, and we discover something we didn't even realize we needed, meet someone we didn't know was missing, or are reached by someone just in time.

When God brings people across our path, He is presenting us with a magnificent gift. More often than not, such a person is instrumental in helping us to achieve a particular goal, which is always a blessing. More importantly, God brings special people into our lives to remind us that we should slow down, pay attention; God is at work in our lives. What seem like coincidences or accidental meetings are purposeful encounters orchestrated by God.

These blessed encounters make us wonder: How often do we miss blessings when we're not watching for His plan?

He alone stretches out the heavens
and treads on the waves of the sea.
He is the Maker of the Bear and Orion,
the Pleiades and the constellations of the south.
He performs wonders that cannot be fathomed,
miracles that cannot be counted.

—Job 9:8–10

VINDICATION

KAMILA BLESSING

When my mother prayed for people, things happened. People used to come to her for prayer all the time. One day during the Vietnam war, a young, recently married couple came to see her. The husband Bill was a marine and had just received his orders to go to Vietnam. He knew this happened to a lot of young people then, but to him his going seemed particularly unjust. Bill had been adopted at birth. For all these years, the idea that his real parents had given him up had been grinding in his stomach. His mother had rejected him and sent him away. He couldn't get past that. It was so unfair. It felt as if he had been judged unworthy to be her son before he even had a chance to do anything at all. Finally, now that he had the chance to form a family of his own, he had to leave and face the front line. He might never come back. It was as if the Father in heaven had abandoned him twice over. He hadn't done anything to deserve this. His heart needed healing badly. His family needed healing too, but he didn't know it yet.

My mother prayed for the couple. After a while, she said, "Go to the hospital chapel, the one with the beautiful stained glass. Go down front and pray and thank God for Vietnam."

"Thank God for Vietnam?" Bill objected. "Not on your life!"

"I'm sorry," Mother replied. "I prayed, and that's what came to me. And that's all I've got."

Bill and his wife weren't at all happy with that, but they were desperate. So they finally reasoned, why not? What could happen? It was, after all, only a prayer.

So they went to the hospital chapel, went down to the front, and, as hard as it was, they thanked God for Vietnam. Once finished with praying, they turned to leave. As they turned, they realized that another couple had entered and were sitting in the back. The husband also had on a Marine uniform. He was clearly an officer.

The two couples began to talk. When they realized that both men had orders to ship out to Vietnam right away, they became more interested in each other. The officer took out some family pictures. "I don't have any except this one of my mother," Bill said. He took out his birthmother's photo, the only thing he had of hers, and gave it to the officer. "I was adopted," Bill explained.

"That can't be your mother," said the officer.

"Why not?"

"Because . . . that's my mother."

It turned out the two were in fact brothers and the mother had to give up Bill for good reasons. In the end, through that unwilling visit to the chapel, the biological family was reunited. The officer requested that Bill work with him in Vietnam, and during that tour of duty, they got to know each other better. Both returned—Bill to be reunited with his wife, and with the family that God had given him.

WHAT ON EARTH IS SHOO-FLY PIE, ANYWAY?

MARY HELEN LIVINGSTON

The doctor closed his bag and turned to me. "Call me if he gets any worse this afternoon or tonight. I'll stop by in the morning to see him. If he's no better, I'll have to put him in the hospital. He needs fluids, and he must eat."

"I've given him everything I can think of, but he just can't keep anything down," I said.

"You must keep on trying. He is getting weak and dehydrated. Do your best. I'll see you tomorrow morning."

I sat down in the rocking chair by the sofa where my little son lay. Bobby had always been thin and undersized; now, after days of battling an especially severe form of influenza, he looked wan and wasted. What would I do if he had to be hospitalized? I was a nursing student at Florida State University in Tallahassee and had no hospitalization insurance and very little money. What if the hospital refused to admit him? I prayed silently, "Lord, show me what to do."

"Bobby, suppose I go to the store and buy a different kind of soup for you. And maybe some Jell-O. Don't you think you might be able to eat some?"

"No, Mama."

"Can't you think of anything you'd like?"

"Make me some shoo-fly pie, Mama. I could eat that. I know I could."

Bobby had never eaten shoo-fly pie in his life. He could not desire something he had never seen or tasted. Yet I knew why he had asked. To pass the long, weary hours of illness, I had been reading stories to him from library books. *Yonie Wondernose* by Marguerite De Angeli was his favorite. It was the story of Johnny, a little Amish boy from the Pennsylvania Dutch area, and it described vividly the customs, dress, food and daily activities of the Amish.

My life had been spent in Georgia and Florida. I knew nothing of the Amish, had never seen an Amish person, had never tasted a Pennsylvania Dutch dish. What on earth *is* shoo-fly pie, anyway? A fruit pie? A custard pie? A savory meat concoction like a shepherd's pie? The little story had mentioned shoo-fly pie, but had failed to list the ingredients. I doubted the wisdom of experimenting with strange, exotic foods in the middle of a serious illness. However, it was the only food Bobby had requested, and maybe it was worth trying. Whatever was in it, it was probably not going to stay in him long enough to do any harm.

Having made the decision to act on Bobby's request, I set about locating a recipe. The Leon County Library did not have a book on Pennsylvania Dutch cookery; neither did the State Library. The library at Florida State University had such a cookbook, but it was in use and not due back for two weeks. I called nearby bookstores.

They had no Pennsylvania Dutch cookbooks. I called my neighbors, friends, relatives. Some of them had heard of shoo-fly pie; none of them knew what it was.

"Bobby, there isn't a recipe for shoo-fly pie in this town. I'm just as sorry as I can be. After you are well, we will try again, but right now we are going to have to do with what we can get. I'm going to the grocery store now and try to find something easy to eat for you. Your grandfather will sit with you while I'm gone."

"What store are you going to Mama? I'll ask God to send you a recipe there. He'll send one."

"Oh, no, Bobby," I said in alarm, "please don't do that!" I couldn't bear the thought of his faith being shattered. And there was obviously no way for God to provide a recipe in a grocery store. I had already tried all the likely places. It would be best for Bobby not to ask for the impossible.

"God will know how to send you a recipe, Mama. Are you going to Winn-Dixie?"

"Yes, I'm going to Winn-Dixie. Don't ask God, honey. I'll be back soon with something good."

In Winn-Dixie I pushed my shopping cart, filling it with red and green Jell-O, butterscotch pudding, chicken noodle soup. And then, nearing the checkout counter, I stood still, not believing what I saw. Walking in the door were two women, one wearing a black prayer cap, the other a white one, just like the pictures in *Yonie Wondernose*. Hurrying toward them, I asked, "Are you Amish?"

"Yes, we are Amish."

"And do you know how to make shoo-fly pie?"

"Of course. All Amish women know how to make shoo-fly pie."

"Could you write me a recipe?"

"Why, yes, certainly. If you have paper, I'll write it down, and then we will help you find the things you need to make a nice pie."

As we walked around gathering brown sugar, molasses, and spices, I asked them if they lived in Tallahassee.

"Oh, goodness no! We are just passing through. We have been down in Florida and are on our way back home to Pennsylvania. I don't know why we stopped in here, but all of a sudden my companion said, 'Let's stop at that Winn-Dixie.' So here we are. I really don't know why we came in."

Awestruck, humbled and ashamed, I knew why. Bobby had disobeyed me. He had asked—and received.

When I walked into the living room with the groceries, Bobby said, "You got the recipe God sent, didn't you, Mama?"

The recipe made, not one, but two large shoo-fly pies. Bobby ate almost a whole pie during the late afternoon and early evening and drank several cups of weak tea. Moreover, he retained all he ate and drank. The pie, high in carbohydrates, provided energy, and the tea replaced body fluids. By morning, Bobby was able to drink fruit juices and eat poached eggs and toast. His improvement thereafter was rapid and dramatic.

And so, after all these years, there's a letter I want to write:

Dear Amish Ladies:

This story is really a long-overdue letter to you. It should have been written immediately after this incident, which happened so many years ago. Please forgive me for not getting your names and addresses. How could I have been so preoccupied with my problems that I failed to provide myself with the means of thanking you two for the parts you played in this drama?

Perhaps, not knowing the beginning or end of the story, you regarded it as a trivial incident and pushed it away, into the vast storehouse of forgetfulness. I want to jog your memory. You had been on a pleasure trip to Florida with friends and were driving back home. You passed through the business district of Tallahassee, Florida. You were driving north on Monroe Street, the highway to Thomasville, Georgia, when you came to a Winn-Dixie on your right. Do you remember?

I want you to remember because, to me, this was not a happen-stance, a coincidence. Through the years, when my faith has faltered, when cynicism has threatened me, I find myself thinking of a very sick child making a simple request that he knew would be granted. Unlike me, Bobby wasn't concerned with how God was going to go about it; he trusted in His infinite power. It reminds me that I have no right to wish my own human limitations on God, for with God all things are possible. Thank you, dear Amish ladies, for being His messengers.

ABOUT TWENTY-FIVE CENTS

CATHE ODOM

When I was six years old our family moved to New Mexico. My father was in the air force, and we had been stationed in cities all over the world. Our stay in New Mexico was to be a temporary assignment. I was accustomed to making friends quickly and having to say good-bye almost as fast. Sometimes that was very hard.

The first day at my new school in New Mexico I met a little girl named Jenny, and we became fast friends. We met every day for lunch and recess, playing games and sharing secrets as if we had known each other forever.

Then one day after lunch I heard Jenny crying and telling the teacher that someone had taken her twenty-five cents, which was her leftover change after buying her lunch. As I approached to comfort her, she pointed her finger at me and said, "Cathe has it, it's in her desk!"

The teacher asked me to open my desk, which I did very innocently. And there it was—twenty-five cents in my pencil holder. The teacher asked me to return the money to Jenny, and in her mind, the matter was resolved.

I returned to my seat, heartbroken. Why would my best friend say I had stolen from her? I knew it was my twenty-five cents that had been in my pencil holder, and

I knew my mother would ask where it was when I got home from school that day. In those days, a quarter was a lot of money for a child. I just couldn't figure out why someone who I thought was a friend would get me in trouble.

When I got home from school and explained the situation to my mother, she was very disappointed with me. Not even she would believe me. I was terribly hurt and embarrassed, convinced that all the other kids would avoid me now. Worst of all, I had lost my best friend and didn't know what I had done to deserve it.

When I went back to school the next day, Jenny refused to play with me, and so did the other kids. It was very painful and confusing to be so lonely and isolated. Luckily, my father was soon transferred and we moved on. This time I was glad to move; I could start over and make new friends. I never heard from Jenny after that, nor did I ever figure out why she had set me up that day.

Many years later, when I was a grown woman, I sat with some friends and newcomers in a church group in California. We chatted before the official meeting began, and the conversation turned to childhood friendships. One of the newcomers began talking about how, as a little girl, she had been constantly scolded by her mother for losing change from her lunch money. She had tried very hard to become more responsible and, in her own young mind, was making some improvements. Then one day at school she realized she had lost her twenty-five cents change from her lunch. Afraid to face her mother, she accused her best friend of taking it.

My eyes grew hot and teary as she continued saying that she would always regret that childish act because she had lost a wonderful friend that day. She had been remorseful her entire life but knew there was nothing she could ever do to make amends.

I listened carefully and watched her now-familiar face closely as she spoke. Finally, I understood why she had done it. She hadn't meant to hurt me—she was just a little child afraid of disappointing her mother!

I remained still throughout the meeting, though it was difficult to focus. I knew I needed to speak with this woman because it was so apparent that the incident had bothered her as much as it had bothered me. After the meeting was over and the other women had left to go to the coffee room, I approached Jenny. "My name is Cathe," I said with a warm smile, and I gently placed a quarter in her hand.

Jenny stared at the quarter and then slowly lifted her head and looked into my face. Tears began to stream down my face. Tears filled her eyes, and we embraced and cried in each other's arms. We were two little girls who had both longed for another chance at friendship, and now, many years later and hundreds of miles from the school yard of our youth, we were able to remember, to forgive and to love again.

It was over thirteen years ago that Jenny and I were brought together in that little church in California. We are still good friends today. We've talked about the miraculous circumstances that allowed us to connect again and that revealed to us the importance of friendship in our lives. And now, when we hear others talk about the value of friends, we jokingly remark that "a real friend is worth just about twenty-five cents!"

MIRACLE ON THE BATTLEFIELD

TOM SHERIDAN

The year was 1944. World War II was at its height. Europe was in flames, and the Allies had begun to slowly wrest back the continent from Hitler. In the Pacific, GIs were slogging from island to island, leaving in their wake the Stars and Stripes, but also wounded and dead comrades. The seas were speckled with ships and battles and heroes.

[Bill] Abbott was a young midshipman in training to be a naval officer. The classes weren't the problem; swimming was. "I couldn't swim," he said. "Not a stroke. And the U.S. Navy frowned upon nonswimmers and absolutely refused to commission anyone who couldn't swim."

He said there were instructors, of course, and they were good. But the final exam was so rigorous that it was very unlikely that someone like me—unable to even take my foot from the bottom—could be raised to the necessary skill level in four short months. My only hope was prayer."

So each morning before his classes, Abbott was at the academy chapel, praying for God's help at the pool during his unavoidable trial by water.

He had delayed the test as long as possible. But the day before graduation, he and another student with the same problem were ordered to the pool. They sat there in regulation blue swimming trunks, recognizing that no matter what else happened, this would be the single test that would determine the course their lives would take. It sounds too much like a cliché, but for these two aspiring naval officers, that day was literally sink or swim.

The testing officer, a lieutenant, called the other cadet first. With an almost visible sense of resignation, he jumped into the chilly water. Despite struggling greatly, he failed. The testing officer told him to report to the academic office. He was through.

It was Abbott's turn. He remembers crossing the slippery tile around the edge of the pool and launching himself off toward the other end. With every stroke came a prayer, and quickly he was praying as hard as he was flailing away at the water. But it was no use. The water seemed to hold him back; the far end of the pool was still far away—too far away.

Finally—his God and his effort notwithstanding—it was over. Halfway through, he couldn't go on. He reached out and grasped the side of the pool, an action by which he automatically disqualified himself. His prayers had failed.

Abbott caught his breath briefly at the edge, then pulled himself out of the pool to report to the testing officer. Certainly, he would quickly follow in the footsteps of the other would-be officer, right out the door. Their conversation went like this:

"Where you from, Abbott?"

"New York, sir."

"I thought so. You sound like a New Yorker. Know any cops, Abbott?"

Abbott had three uncles, all New York City policemen. So he said, "Yes, sir."

"What're their names?"

"Tim, Bill and Ed."

"What's Tim?" the officer asked.

"A detective," Abbott answered.

"He's also one of my best friends," said the lieutenant. "Go back to your section, Abbott, and just make sure you don't fall overboard for the rest of the war."

His prayers were answered—though not as he had expected.

Abbott told me that when he realized afterward what had just happened, he thought, *Had I jumped into the water and swum the distance, maybe my prayers would have worked. Or maybe I would have been able to swim because I was convinced I could. If I had succeeded, it might have been a miracle. Or it might not have been. We'd never know. But I didn't make it. I failed.*

Please note: The testing officer was honest. He didn't say, "You passed." He just sent the young midshipman back to his section. Abbott never heard from him again. "The following day, I graduated with my class and went to sea," he said. During

World War II, there were three hundred and eighty-five thousand officers in the U.S. Navy. What were the odds that one who was my uncle's best friend would be the one to administer my swimming test on that day? It was a minor miracle, to be sure, but one which confirms the awesome power of prayer."

NICE TIMING

THOMAS DEPAOLI

I had spent over five grueling years on my dissertation for my Ph.D. and was frantically preparing for my oral boards. The boards were to be held in California, and I had scheduled a flight through Minneapolis, where I was to change planes and get to John Wayne Airport. My incoming flight was very late, and I was soon in an all-out sprint to catch my flight to California. Very few people were left in the concourse. I had to stop to catch my breath on a moving sidewalk when I noticed a woman in her fifties struggling with a carry-on bag.

I don't know why, but I looked at her face and blurted out, "Are you going on Flight 567 to California?"

She responded, "Yes."

"So am I," I responded. "Give me your bag. I'll run ahead and tell them to wait for you." I took her bag and started sprinting again.

I raced onto the plane and told the flight attendant that one more passenger was behind me and to please hold the plane for her. I seated myself with her bag, and a few moments later she arrived and was the last person on the plane before they closed the doors and took off. After the plane leveled off, I presented the bag to her, and she smiled at me and thanked me.

I didn't sleep a wink in the hotel that I stayed at before my oral boards and arrived at the university at seven o'clock in the morning. The board kept me waiting for an hour in a room before the defense of my dissertation began. I walked into the boardroom and was initially intimidated by all the professors in their regal robes. As I slowly glanced at the faces of all the board members, I noticed the bright face of a woman directly in the center of the board. She looked at me, gave me a flirtatious smile like a young schoolgirl and winked at me. It was the same woman whose bag I had carried ahead the night before. Needless to say, whenever I stumbled on any questions, she did a great job of extricating me.

THIS WAY TO PUMPKIN PIE

BOB Y.

One thing we agreed on that crisp fall Sunday was that our supper had to be topped off with fresh, homemade pumpkin pie. It would be the only proper ending for the day we had in mind.

"Pumpkin pie is nonnegotiable," I said, laughing as we drove along a winding country road in the car we had rented back in New York City. We had come upstate to see the brilliant colors of the changing foliage, and we had not been disappointed. Tony, Phil and I had met several years earlier in an Alcoholics Anonymous group in the city. Back then we were new to AA. Together we had found sobriety and learned how to ask God for help. From time to time we liked to get together outside AA to share the new direction God was giving our lives.

But on this day our own sense of direction was far from perfect, for during the amiable debate over what, when and where our old-fashioned country meal would be, we got lost. As the driver, I was being held responsible, and unfortunately the rental car had not come equipped with a New York State road map.

"Maybe God wants to guide us after all," concluded Tony with a chuckle, trying to get me off the hook.

"It's obviously out of *your* hands," chided Phil, tapping me on the shoulder from the backseat.

Eventually we did come to a little inn. We were ushered to a table in the dining room, where a fire crackled in the fireplace, and paintings of George Washington adorned the walls. We agreed that this was exactly what we had had in mind. And they advertised fresh pumpkin pie.

"Something from the bar, gentlemen?" inquired our young waitress. She seemed nervous. *Maybe it's her first day on the job*, I thought.

"A round of Cokes," Tony said. We nodded our approval. The waitress smiled.

Over appetizers we joked about how important food had become for us in sobriety. "After my first year of not drinking," remarked Phil, "my taste buds came back. Now if I want a drink, I pick up a pizza instead."

Our waitress hovered around the table, cleaning ashtrays we had not used and filling our water glasses after nearly every sip. *This* has *to be her first day or something*, I thought again.

Finally she left us to devour our dinner of roast duck and almond chicken, wild rice, and steamed vegetables. As soon as our plates were cleared, we were ready for that pumpkin pie. But our waitress shook her head sadly. The last of the lot had just been served.

"We have great apple pie, homemade pecan pie, Indian pudding . . ."

It was no use. We really wanted pumpkin pie.

The way we groaned you would have thought we had just been informed that pumpkins were suddenly extinct. Without a word, the waitress turned on her heel and left. We sat sheepishly stirring our coffee.

"Don't tell anyone," she whispered a few minutes later as she put three pieces of pumpkin pie before us. "The cooks were saving these for themselves, but I talked them out of it. I told them it was important."

"Thanks," I muttered self-consciously, now rather embarrassed.

"No, thank *you*," she said, smiling warmly. "You guys don't know what you've done for me today." We looked bewildered, then she came closer. "I'm in AA, too. I'm new at it and it's been pretty tough. I've just been trying to hang on. All day I've been praying and praying for strength, and asking God to tell me everything's going to be all right, that I don't have to pick up a drink. Then out of nowhere you guys appear and a table just happens to open up in my section." She paused to catch her breath. "Just when I was feeling lost, you found me. Thanks." And then she was off to another table.

We were silent for a while. There it was again, another example of how God is always there to show us the way when we ask for directions. And sometimes when we don't.

We cut into our pie. I wasn't surprised to find it was the best pumpkin pie I had ever tasted.

STRANGE DAY AT LAKE MUNKAMBA

WILLIAM F. PRUITT

Kasai Province, Zaire, Africa. 1968. As one of the missionaries who had been allowed to return to his former station in what was once the Belgian Congo, I'd been "itinerating" for several weeks—that is, visiting among the tribal missions in a radius of about a hundred miles of my station in Moma. One evening, after preaching and showing Cecil B. DeMille's 1927 classic film, *King of Kings*, I found that I was only about thirty miles from our house on Lake Munkamba.

Almost on impulse I decided to spend the night there. It was late, after eleven, and I was very tired. But I was also tired of sleeping in my house-truck. Besides, I wanted to see the house again.

This was no ordinary house. I don't mean architecturally, though that too, given the local standards. It was extraordinary because it was *ours*—the only home in Africa that was our very own. We had built it years before as a hideaway for little family vacations, and now, with Virginia and our two sons far away in America, I longed even more to go there. The house represented home and love and a security that often seemed elusive in those days of internal African strife. I needed to be reminded of these qualities once more.

As I drove toward the lake, I wondered in what condition I'd find our hideaway this time. During the tribal fighting of the early 1960s, it had been looted frequently. Doors and windows and most of the furnishings—as well as the much-coveted tin roof—had been carried away. Our roof now covered the local chief's hut, but he had explained his taking it. "When I saw those looters taking everything from your house," he had said, "I knew you would want me instead of them to have that tin roof!" Logic against which I could offer no rebuke.

At last I arrived. The house was still there. I fumbled my way in the darkness through the bare living room to a cot in one of the bedrooms and fell onto it. Exhausted, I was soon asleep.

I awakened early the next morning, looked about a little, and said my prayers. I thanked God for another day of life and asked Him to watch over me. Outside, through the morning mist, I saw a lone native fisherman on the shore nearby. There seemed to be no one else about. All was quiet. African quiet.

Time to get going, I told myself, and took my five-gallon jerry can to the spring and filled it with drinking water. Back at the house, I picked up my hat, and was about to leave when I caught sight of the fisherman again. It made me wish I had time to join him for a quick catch. *Well, someday*, I thought. *I'd just better check to see if that outboard motor I left last summer is still here.* With so much looting, there was no telling what might have become of a prize like an outboard motor.

I put down the jerry can and went to a small storeroom in the back of the house. It was windowless and gloomy inside, but I could see that the motor was still there. *That's a relief,* I thought, reaching down and patting it as if to say, "Good boy! Stay there, because you and I have some fishing to catch up on as soon as I can get a day off!"

At just that moment I became aware of something else in a corner of the room. It was black and coiled into a circle, as though very carefully placed there. *I don't remember having a rope like that,* I said to myself. I went over to have a closer look. I went *too* close.

Oh! Oh, dear Lord!

Zoom!

I felt a spray of liquid; it was as though a red-hot nail had been driven through my right eye!

Instantly I knew that what I had taken for a coiled rope was a spitting cobra, one of the most poisonous snakes in the world!

I screamed out loud and started running, running away, but I no sooner got to the door than I stumbled over the jerry can of water. Quickly I threw myself down on all fours and frantically splashed cold water into my face, trying to put out the fire that was spreading through my head.

A figure loomed over me. "*Maumbi!** What is the matter?" It was the fisherman from the lake.

He looked at me, looked at the room, and ran away. *He knows what has happened,* I told myself. *He knows there's nothing he can do. He's probably gone to tell the chief that I'm here and dying.* Every native African knows that the spitting cobra first blinds and paralyzes its victim with a deadly venom before attacking again.

The pain was excruciating. Where was the snake now? I went on splashing water on my face even though I knew my flailing might cause it to strike again.

Was I beginning to feel a numbing sensation creeping over me? It seemed that way, but I wasn't sure.

Minutes went by, maybe five, maybe ten. Three people entered the room. Strangers. A man and two women, white.

The man rushed to me. "What's happened?" he asked, and I stuttered out the word, "Cobra."

He ran outside and came back with a large stick. "There it is!" he yelled, as he lifted the stick and again and again brought it down on the snake's head, killing the creature—a seven-foot-long female carrying seven eggs!

One of the women came to me, checked my pulse, and tried to look into my

---

*"Preacher" or "Missionary" in the Tshiluba language.

blinded eye. "I'm a nurse," she said. Then she looked up at the other two people helplessly. "I don't know what to do, but I feel I *must* do something! Then, as almost an afterthought, she opened her handbag and started searching for something. "A sample of an eye medication came to me in the mail the other day. I don't know anything about it," she said, addressing me, "but it's all we have. Shall I try it on you?"

I understood what she was really saying: the poor man is going to die anyway—or go blind; why not take the gamble?

I nodded and she put a few drops of the unknown prescription in my eye.

"It's just possible that the water you threw on your face helped," the nurse said. Now we waited to give the medication time to do its work, if it was going to.

A half hour passed. Just as the pain seemed to be easing, we heard footsteps. Another white man appeared, a stranger to the others. I was mystified. Where were all these people coming from? In those days in that part of Africa, no unidentified white man traveled alone.

Who was he? A French doctor, he said, on his way to a diamond mine fifty miles away. He'd heard of the beautiful Lake Munkamba and he'd detoured several miles off his route, parked his car a half mile away, and walked down to the shore of the lake.

The nurse explained to him what had happened to me. "Do you know how to treat venom in the eye?" she asked.

"Yes," he answered. He told us of an effective new antibiotic. In fact, he had used it successfully on a man at the diamond mine just the month before. Unfortunately, he didn't have any with him.

"Do you know anything about this?" the nurse asked, handing him the medication she had put in my eye.

He looked at it carefully. "That's it! That's it! That's the very one I was telling you about!"

The French doctor stayed for a while. Then, after giving instructions for applying the drops every thirty minutes and telling me to stay in bed for the next twenty-four hours, he left us, as quickly and mysteriously as he had arrived. None of us had even learned his name!

Now, however, I learned who my other saviors were: a Scottish missionary and his wife who were vacationing nearby and a nurse visiting them from an English mission. The kindly Scotsman took me to his house and put me to bed.

The next morning my eyesight was fully restored, my energy had returned, and my eye was not even red! Today I see as well from one eye as from the other.

But for the rest of that long day, and throughout the longer dark hours of the night, I lay reliving everything that had happened. It was easy enough to keep my body quiet, as the doctor had directed, but stilling the flow of emotion was impossible.

I prayed, of course, thanking God for His unfailing mercy and grace. I thanked Him for all of those who had had a part in my recovery and what I earnestly believed would be the restoration of my sight. I whistled hymns through my teeth and was relieved to feel no facial paralysis.

In the assurance of God's presence, I also slept. But during waking hours I played a game of "what if." What if:

...I hadn't gone for water before checking the storeroom?

...the fisherman had been on another part of the lake?

...the missionaries and their guest hadn't been visiting?

...the guest hadn't been a nurse?

...there had been no sample of a new antibiotic in her purse?

...the doctor had not appeared?

And so on and so on. This "what if" game went on endlessly.

And yet, I knew it wasn't a game at all. I knew that all of us at Lake Munkamba that morning had been participants with God in yet another of His unfathomable deeds. Had I been the object of an extraordinary series of coincidences? No, absolutely not. For in God's world, there are no coincidences.

Chapter 3   Timely Provision

Most of us have experienced God's blessing of provision in food and shelter, family and friends. But sometimes we find ourselves in situations of need for which the usual solutions just don't suffice. When a harvest fails or a car breaks down, a child's Christmas wish is left unanswered or in even more dire situations, every solution we imagine for the problem fails. Nothing we try works.

We're then faced with trying to cope with the results of our existing circumstances, trying to imagine how to do without. Sometimes it's only a temporary setback, a minor disappointment, but other times the well-being of our family, even the life of someone we love, is at stake.

And just when things seem hopeless, when we've exhausted all the possibilities, God's grace enters with a sense of wonder as He provides for us in a way we cannot possibly provide for ourselves. He supplies our needs, specifically and generously, and in the most creative, unexpected ways. This provision is often called good fortune, a coincidence of cosmic proportions. We smile and shake our heads, even laugh out loud at the irony or the odds. But we can also marvel at God's great love and concern for our every need. Just look how He clothes the lilies of the field.

I was young and now I am old,
yet I have never seen the righteous forsaken
or their children begging bread.
They are always generous and lend freely;
their children will be blessed.

—Psalm 37:25–26

CAR TROUBLE

RON BAILEY

The other day my wife and I were talking with a neighbor, and the subject of feeling close to God came up. Immediately I thought of a time years ago, a time of great uncertainty for Carolyn and me. It was early in our marriage. Carolyn was eighteen, I was twenty-two, and our first child, Karen, was a year old. I had just finished my tour of duty with the Navy in San Diego, and we were heading home to Tacoma, Washington.

Packing and getting on the road had worn us out. We had only enough money for gas and groceries. My separation check from the Navy would be mailed to my folks' home in Tacoma. *And then what?* we wondered. I had no trade, no job. How would we get by? This was in our minds and in our conversation on the road back home. Frankly, there weren't any answers, and that was scary.

"I'm exhausted," I said to Carolyn.

"Me too," she replied wearily as she tried to soothe our fretting baby girl.

Dusk had fallen in the Siskiyou Mountains. Pulling our eight-year-old business coupe into a clearing by the roadside, we camped for the night in the twenty-one-foot trailer hitched behind the car. The trailer had been our home in California, and we were pulling it to Tacoma with us.

We were miles from any town, along a two-lane road that led through the mountains of northern California. Not much traffic passed along this stretch except for an occasional truck whizzing—a little too fast, I thought—around the curves.

Early the next morning, just after breakfast, I noticed it: an old black Buick sedan stopped right at the end of the road. "What a strange place for anyone to stop," I said to Carolyn. "You'd think the driver would know better."

The car was half on, half off the road. No one could pass without going into the opposite lane. And one of those big trucks might be coming around the bend. . . .

"Carolyn, I'm going to go up and speak to those people about moving their car." I had seen a man get out and go to the back of the car, then a woman. As I approached, they both looked frustrated. Hopeless, you might say. A boy of about six was looking out of the window.

"This is a dangerous stopping point," I called out.

"I can't get it to move," the man said to me. "It just locked up. I think it's this back wheel. But I tell you, it won't move."

"Well, maybe you should try pushing it off the road."

"It won't move," he said again helplessly.

"Got any tools?" I asked the man.

"Well, no, ah . . . I'm not very mechanical, I'm afraid. We're on our way to

Oregon, where I have a job prospect. This couldn't have happened at a worse time."

All of their possessions were inside the car and strapped on top of it. It was clear that this young family had been struggling. Everything about them spoke of their need. The old car. Well-worn clothes. Belongings that most people would sell at a yard-sale. That job prospect was their only hope, and now, with barely enough money for gas, they were faced with car trouble.

I directed the man to go up the road and the woman to go down the road to warn approaching traffic. Then I got my tools, jacked up the Buick, and took off the rear wheel.

The brake linings had wedged over one another and had forced the round drum into an ellipse that was locked in place. I forced off the brake drum with a pry bar and hammer. Brake drum, brake shoes, lining—all useless. Then I bolted the wheel back on, and we coasted the car down to our trailer so that I could work on it.

It would take some sort of invention to put this family, desperate to get to that job interview, back on the road. "The best I can do," I said to the man and his wife, "is to pinch off the brake tube to this wheel so you won't lose fluid when you press the brake pedal. That means you'll have three wheels with brakes and one without. That will get you to the nearest town, but you must stop there and replace the drum and brake shoes."

I could see the worried looks cross their faces. I figured the reason—they didn't have the money for parts or repairs. "Do you have any relatives or friends in this part of the country?" I asked.

"No," said the man. "No one."

Carolyn and I didn't have much either, but at least we were heading toward family.

"Well, on this mountain road you can't drive very far with only three working brakes. It's just too dangerous . . ." I still hadn't figured how I would close off the brake tube to that one wheel. Maybe I could make something to cap it—or pinch it shut. As I was considering possibilities, the couple's little boy ran up. He'd been playing just down the bank.

"Daddy, Daddy—" In his excitement he could hardly get his breath. "There's a car down the bank, and it's just like ours!"

"Oh, son," said his father, a bit wearily, "it may look like ours, but it isn't." His mind was far away, somewhere up the road, at the next town, wondering how he was going to buy the parts he needed to get them to Oregon.

"Son, you just think it looks like ours. Now you run and play. We've got to fix this car somehow."

"But Daddy, it is just like ours!"

He was so positive that I said to the man, "Why don't we just have a look? It couldn't hurt."

The car was overturned about sixty feet down the embankment, and as we climbed down I could see that it had landed near some large boulders near a river. The engine and transmission were missing—taken by scavengers. So were the wheels.

But as I inspected it, the man and I looked at each other. Our curiosity turned to wonder. The car was *identical* to his. Same model, same year, same color. And though the wheels were missing, the brake drums were still intact.

I had brought my pry bar and hammer and some wrenches, and I busied myself in taking off the brake drum that was closest. I was balancing on the rocks and working with the wrenches while the man and his son poked around the car.

"Could I borrow that pry bar?" the man asked.

"Sure," I said and handed it over.

Intent on my work and still thinking about the coincidence of an identical wreck being at the exact spot in the road where this man's car broke down, I heard the two working with the pry bar to open the trunk of this old hulk. Still locked, or rusted shut after all these years. . . .

Then I heard the creaking sounds of the trunk hinges opening. "Hey, there's a lug wrench!" shouted the man. "I could sure use that . . . and there's a paper bag." I heard the rustling of paper. And then silence.

The man came around to where I was working. He stared at me for a moment. I could tell it was difficult for him to speak. He held a brown paper sack.

"Do you have any idea what's in this sack?" he asked finally.

He stood there swallowing hard, trying not to cry. "Here . . . see? New brake shoes!"

With the necessary parts provided, I repaired their car, Carolyn fixed them a meal, and they started off down the road, waving. Alone? Helpless? Not at all. You see, I knew that Somebody upstairs cared very much for those three, and He was providing for their every need.

Right then and there, things no longer seemed so uncertain for Carolyn and me and Karen, either. For I also knew that if God could provide for those people, He could provide for us.

And as I was telling my neighbor the other day, for all these years, He has done just that.

THE CHRISTMAS EVE GIFT

MARY WELKER

No one wants to pull hospital duty on Christmas Eve—or on Christmas Day either, for that matter. To be parted from your loved ones on a holiday, to miss the festivities that are taking place in your absence, is difficult indeed. But what makes the assignment that much more wrenching for hospital staff is watching the pain and suffering of patients forced to remain in the hospital. The emotional trauma gets compounded when you consider the tragic fate of many of these gravely ill patients: For several, this is the very last holiday in their lives.

Working as I do in a children's hospital, Christmas duty can be both a heartbreaking and heartwarming experience. But when I drew the assignment for both Christmas Eve and Christmas Day, I tried to make the best of it. We hosted a visit by a merry Santa Claus who spread cheer throughout the hospital as he distributed gifts to delighted youngsters, and we stuffed stockings with toys that the patients would wake up to the following morning.

As I and several other Childlife Specialists worked busily in the staff office, someone knocked loudly on the door (we wanted the stockings to be a surprise for the children, so we were vigilant about keeping the door shut). It was a teenage patient who was familiar to us all. He had been in and out of the hospital several times during the past year, and we had grown very fond of him. Despite his own serious condition, he was a very warm and generous-hearted boy. He always took the time to scoop the younger patients up in his arms and give them rides in his wheelchair, read bedtime stories to them, or initiate water-gun fights on the floor, which distracted the children and filled them with glee.

Johnny had just been readmitted to the hospital that night and had come to our office to offer his help in stuffing the stockings. We were taken aback that this feisty teenager had allowed himself to be admitted—of all times!—on Christmas Eve. Why hadn't he waited until the following morning? we inquired. Didn't he want to stay home with his family and open presents?

A sad expression stole over Johnny's face. "No," he answered, "it would be worse for me to stay home."

He explained that his parents would give him things he didn't care about or particularly need. "They'll give me clothes and CDs and other stuff, and while I appreciate their kindness," he said, "it's not what I want."

"What *do* you want?" we asked, hoping against hope that it was something we had already heaped in one of the stocking stuffers.

"A Nintendo Sixty-four," he answered.

Our shoulders sagged in disappointment. It was certainly not among the items we had amassed in our office. We gently reminded him that the Nintendo 64—the hottest-selling Christmas item that year—was not only difficult to get, but expensive, too.

"I know," he said wistfully. "It's just that I thought if I would get a Nintendo Sixty-four, then maybe my brothers would stay home more often and play the games with me, instead of dashing out the door all the time and leaving me alone."

Our hearts broke for Johnny, and if there had been anyplace open at 10:00 P.M. Christmas Eve, we would have zipped around the hospital collecting money from the staff, hurtled out the door, and bought him one immediately. Needless to say, however, every single store in our neighborhood was closed. When we quit our shift for the night, we returned home with a sad, empty feeling inside. We felt that somehow we had let Johnny down by not being able to fulfill his one—and maybe last—holiday wish.

Christmas morning, my department beeper went off at 6:30 A.M. Surprised, I called in to see what was up, and the secretary in the emergency room said that she was going off duty and wanted to give me a gift that had been dropped off during the night. I told her that I would be in about 8:00 A.M. and asked her to open the wrappings in order to determine whether the gift should be left at Security or remain in the ER. She could not fathom why I started sobbing on the phone when she told me the gift was a Nintendo 64. I have never cried so hard in my whole life.

"How did it get to the emergency room?" I sniffled a few minutes later, when my sobs finally began to subside.

"Some people dropped it off at about one o'clock this morning," she said. "They figured the emergency room is open round-the-clock, so it's accessible. They asked us to give it to a patient in the hospital who would enjoy it."

There are no words to describe Johnny's face when he opened that package or his smile as his brothers sat with him in his room for hours playing Nintendo. We were so touched that we shared the story with everyone in the hospital that day. We felt sad that the people who helped make this miracle happen were unaware of the amazing thing they had done. We decided to try to track them down.

I rummaged through the bag in which the Nintendo had been dropped off and found a credit card receipt with a person's name on it. I called information and found a listing for the name. A woman answered the phone, and when I asked if she was the one who had dropped off the Nintendo the previous night, she answered yes. Together, she and her son had stopped at the hospital with the gift.

How had they come to bring a Nintendo 64? I asked casually, noting that it was quite an unusual and expensive gift to donate to a hospital.

"Oh, it's a long story," she said.

"Please tell me," I begged.

"Well," she began, "my son is engaged to a woman who lives in a different state. She has two boys by a previous marriage, and they both wanted a Nintendo 64 for Christmas. Because the toy was so popular, it wasn't readily available in the small town where she lives, so she asked my son to try to get one for her here. He, too, experienced difficulty in obtaining one—it seems to be quite a hot item this year— and he told her on the phone that he had not been successful as yet, but would certainly keep on trying. When he called her a few days ago to announce triumphantly 'Mission accomplished!'—he had finally bought one—she laughed and said she had just bought one too, that very same day! So now he had an extra Nintendo 64 on his hands, which he placed in the car so he would remember to return it to the store.

"We were returning from the services last night when I noticed the Nintendo on his back seat. I asked him what he was planning to do with the extra one, and he said, 'Return it eventually when I get the time.' Just then we happened to be passing the Children's Hospital so I impulsively said: 'How about donating it to a sick child, instead?'"

I told the woman a little bit about Johnny, the patient who had been the thrilled recipient of her special generosity. She asked me about his illness, and I told her he had cancer. She started to cry. Then she asked me what type. When I answered, she cried even harder. She told me that she herself had been diagnosed with the same type of cancer a year before, and she had undergone a very rough time with the debilitating treatments.

She had suggested to her son that they donate the Nintendo 64 to the Children's Hospital because of her tremendous empathy for the little patients confined there. If she, as an adult, had had such a hard time, she told her son, imagine how tough it must be for a child.

We used to have a lot of skeptics on staff at the hospital. We now have an inordinate number of brand-new believers, who have witnessed firsthand how wonderfully connected all of us are by the spirit of friendship and love.

And I am very glad, after all, that I drew hospital duty that shift, so that I could witness this wondrous miracle myself.

PERFECT TIMING

JOAN WESTER ANDERSON

How do we know when God answers a prayer? Rarely does He communicate with trumpet blasts or skywriting. However, there are those moments when a response is so immediate, so explicit, that it couldn't be anyone *but* God. . . .

As a single parent, Debra Bredican struggled to raise a small daughter in a one-bedroom apartment in suburban Chicago. To supplement her salary, she made health-food dinners for friends. Her client base grew as satisfied customers spread the word about Debra's tasty menus.

Debra dreamed of expanding, but she would need a second bedroom for an office, plus an apartment manager who would let her install a second refrigerator. Both seemed impossible goals. She couldn't afford more than a six hundred and fifty dollar monthly rental—too modest for the area she had in mind. And buying a second refrigerator would take all her savings. Was it too risky? Debra talked it over with God. "If you want me to do this," she told Him, "You'll have to figure it out."

Soon Debra found an apartment complex in a perfect location. But the two-bedroom rents were too expensive. She kept looking—and praying—and occasionally checked back with the complex.

"You're in luck," the rental agent told her one day. "Because of renovations, we're lowering rents on all two-bedroom units for the next six months."

"How much will they be?" Debra scarcely dared to ask.

"Six hundred and fifty-two dollars," the agent answered.

Debra was *almost* convinced that this was God's answer. But there was one more thing. "I'm expanding my home business," she told the agent. "I'm going to need an apartment with two refrigerators."

"Two refrigerators?" The woman laughed. "That's just about impossible. But let me see what I can do."

Debra went home, almost afraid to hope. But the next day, the agent phoned. "This is odd, Debra," she began. "Remember I told you we're in the middle of a huge remodeling job?"

Debra remembered.

"Well, we ordered two hundred and twenty new refrigerators. Yesterday they delivered two hundred and twenty-one. It will be cheaper for us to put the extra in your apartment than to send it back."

Debra had no more doubts. Today her business is thriving, thanks to prayers answered at just the right time.

ANGEL IN UNIFORM

JEANNIE ECKE SOWELL

This is a family story my father told me about his mother, my grandmother. In 1949, my father had just returned home from the war. On every American highway you could see soldiers in uniform hitchhiking home to their families, as was the custom at that time in America.

Sadly, the thrill of his reunion with his family was soon overshadowed. My grandmother became very ill and had to be hospitalized. It was her kidneys, and the doctors told my father that she needed a blood transfusion immediately or she would not live through the night. The problem was that Grandmother's blood type was AB–, a very rare type even today, but even harder to get then because there were no blood banks or air flights to ship blood. All the family members were typed, but not one member was a match. So the doctors gave the family no hope, my grandmother was dying.

My father left the hospital in tears to gather up all the family members, so that everyone would get a chance to tell Grandmother good-bye. As my father was driving down the highway, he passed a soldier in uniform hitchhiking home to his family. Deep in grief, my father had no inclination at that moment to do a good deed. Yet it was almost as if something outside himself pulled him to a stop, and he waited as the stranger climbed into the car.

My father was too upset to even ask the soldier his name, but the soldier noticed my father's tears right away and inquired about them. Through his tears, my father told this total stranger that his mother was lying in a hospital dying because the doctors had been unable to locate her blood type, AB–, and if they did not locate her blood type before nightfall, she would surely die.

It got very quiet in the car. Then this unidentified soldier extended his hand out to my father, palm up. Resting in the palm of his hand were the dog tags form around his neck. The blood type on the tags was AB–. The soldier told my father to turn the car around and get him to the hospital.

My grandmother lived until 1996, forty-seven years later, and to this day no one in our family knows the soldier's name. But my father has often wondered, was he a soldier or an angel in uniform?

A COINCIDENCE?

ED KOPER

I was very proud of my daughter Emily. At only nine years old, she had been carefully saving her allowance money and trying to earn extra money by doing small jobs around the neighborhood. Emily was determined to save enough to buy a girl's mountain bike, an item for which she'd been longing, and she'd been faithfully putting her money away since the beginning of the year.

"How're you doing, honey?" I asked soon after Thanksgiving. I knew she had hoped to have all the money she needed by the end of the year.

"I have forty-nine dollars, Daddy," she said. "I'm not sure if I'm going to make it."

"You've worked so hard, " I said encouragingly. "Keep it up. But you know that you can have your pick from my bicycle collection."

"Thanks, Daddy. But your bikes are so *old*."

I smiled to myself because I knew she was right. As a collector of vintage bicycles, all my girls' bikes were 1950s models—not the kind a kid would choose today.

When the Christmas season arrived, Emily and I went comparison shopping, and she saw several less expensive bikes for which she thought she'd have to settle. As we left one store, she noticed a Salvation Army volunteer ringing his bell by a big kettle. "Can we give them something, Daddy?" she asked.

"Sorry, Em, I'm out of change," I replied.

Emily continued to work hard all through December, and it seemed she might make her goal after all. Then suddenly one day, she came downstairs to the kitchen and made an announcement to her mother.

"Mom," she said hesitantly, "you know all the money I've been saving?"

"Yes, dear," smiled my wife Diane.

"God told me to give it to the poor people."

Diane knelt down to Emily's level. "That's a very kind thought, sweetheart. But you've been saving all year. Maybe you could give *some* of it."

Emily shook her head vigorously. "God said *all.*"

When we saw she was serious, we gave her various suggestions about where she could contribute. But Emily had received specific instructions, and so one cold Sunday morning before Christmas, with little fanfare, she handed her total savings of fifty-eight dollars to a surprised and grateful Salvation Army volunteer.

Moved by Emily's selflessness, I suddenly noticed that a local car dealer was collecting used bicycles to refurbish and give to poor children for Christmas. And I realized that if my nine-year-old daughter could give away all her money, I could certainly give up one bike from my collection.

As I picked up a shiny but old-fashioned kid's bike from the line in the garage, it seemed as if a second bicycle in the line took on a glow. Should I give a *second* bike? No, certainly the one would be enough.

But as I got to my car, I couldn't shake the feeling that I should donate that second bike as well. And if Emily could follow heavenly instructions, I decided I could, too. I turned back and loaded the second bike into the trunk, then took off for the dealership.

When I delivered the bikes, the car dealer thanked me and said, "you're making two kids very happy, Mr. Koper. And here are your tickets."

"Tickets?" I asked.

"Yes. For each bike donated, we're giving away one chance to win a brand-new men's twenty-one-speed mountain bike from a local bike shop. So here are your tickets for two chances."

Why wasn't I surprised when the second ticket won the bike? "I can't believe you won!" laughed Diane, delighted.

"I didn't," I said. "It's pretty clear that Emily did."

And why wasn't I surprised when the bike dealer happily substituted a gorgeous new girl's mountain bike for the man's bike advertised?

Coincidence? Maybe. I like to think it was God's way of rewarding a little girl for a sacrifice beyond her years—while giving her dad a lesson in charity and the power of the Lord.

THE SUDDEN FREEZE

AGNES HUYSER

When my husband Quincy and I bought a farm and moved to Gallatin Gateway in April some years ago, I couldn't wait to get unpacked. I had to plant my vegetable garden by May.

I needed some extra confidence this time, since I had never planted a garden so close to the mountains before and I wasn't "onto" the sudden nighttime temperature changes that wreak havoc on plants.

I enjoyed planting a big garden, but I also felt it was a necessity. With thirteen growing children to feed, I had to make my contribution to our family's health and finances. My garden would provide us with enough vegetables for canning to see us through the next winter.

Quincy and the boys worked hard on our five hundred acres, tending the beef and milk cows, chickens and pigs. The girls and I cultivated the garden, planted seeds, weeded and watered. There was hardly a vegetable in a seed catalog for our altitude that I didn't have in my garden.

Our new home abutted the foot hills of snow-capped peaks seventy miles from Yellowstone National Park. I looked forward to a family outing there to see the roaring waterfalls, the hot spouting geysers, the cold sparkling rivers, and the antelope, elk, and other wildlife.

We were now also only ten miles from my mom and dad. Their deep faith had rubbed off on me, and when I poked a tiny carrot seed in the soft earth, I felt the Lord kneeling right beside me, getting His knees and hands dirty too. I thought I had a no-fail crop-insurance policy.

True, I put in long hours, and when canning season arrived, I'd often be working till midnight canning tomatoes, beans or whatever was ripe at the time. But I really enjoyed it, and I knew that when winter came, I'd be able to go down to the cellar to get three or four quarts of vegetables for supper. I'd linger and feast my eyes on the thousand-plus quarts of ruby red beets, green beans, golden corn, peas, carrots and strawberries, to name a few, that I had provided for my family.

By August I knew my garden would be a winner again; one hundred fifty quarts of green beans were already canned and on the shelves. We always did the beans "assembly line"—I'd pick the tender vines, and the girls would cut and snap, joking and talking non-stop under the old willow tree in the yard. The deep satisfaction I felt packing away the jars and processing made the hot, steamy job worth every bead of sweat.

Making pickles was next, and *that* job was a real labor of love. Our kids insisted I pack a pickle in their school lunches, and if I forgot, I'd hear about it. Deep down, I was flattered. That summer, though, the dill came up poorly, yellowish and unfit for pickling. I blamed it on the black gumbo soil. But Mom and Dad had plenty of "volunteer" dill that had resown itself, so by late August I placed an SOS phone call.

"Mom, I have a terrific crop of cucumbers! Can you spare some dill for pickles?"

They drove up before I had a chance to pick the cucumbers. The kids had already scattered to the pasture, well into their usual after-supper baseball game. Mom carried in a big brown paper bag full to bulging with the most beautiful green dill I had ever seen. She set it down in the entryway, and we visited and watched the kids in the field. At dusk the folks drove off.

"I'll pick the cukes first thing in the morning," I yawned at Quincy. "It's too dark out in the garden now."

But I never did get to pick them. The next morning as I neared the garden, I stopped in my tracks when I saw the devastation before me. A hard freeze had stolen in during the night. Yesterday's firm, perky cucumber leaves were like limp, wet rags, hiding soft mushy cucumbers below. The patch was a total loss.

I hurried to the staked-up tomatoes. Yesterday they were green and some were turning, ready to be brought inside to ripen. Today they too were mushy, black and glassy.

I was heartsick. This was a tremendous loss to our food supply. And all that time and effort wasted! I felt I had let the family and myself down. If only I'd stayed up and listened to the weather report on the late news. Truth is, even if I had remembered, I had been too tired.

I berated myself all day for not having gone out and picked the cucumbers by flashlight. And that night, I tossed and turned, feeling quite alone, though Quincy was sleeping peacefully beside me. Despite my carefully nurtured faith in the Lord, I wasn't accepting this disappointment gracefully. The Lord knew how hard I had worked to do the right thing by my family.

Like a broken record, I was tormenting myself with if-onlys when I heard a gentle voice saying, "Agnes, who feeds you and your family?" Was I hearing things? Everyone else was asleep. Then I decided it could be only one Person speaking to me.

I paused before whispering weakly, "Well, God, You do." Then I added as if to affirm my faith, "I know it all comes from You."

It was a while before the voice continued, "Does it really matter if it comes out of your garden or not?"

That question took me by surprise, and I giggled. "God, I guess it doesn't really matter whether or not it comes from my garden. I know it all comes from You." With that I was given total peace, and I fell asleep.

The next day I was still puzzled by the Lord's question. For days I hoped someone in the valley would have a bumper crop of cucumbers and I'd be able to fill the pickle jars. But no cucumbers, much less tomatoes, came my way.

Eventually I got tired of looking at the bag of dill mocking me in the entryway. One day I jammed another bag over the top and placed the dill out of sight on a roughed-in ledge by the stairs leading to the cellar.

The following winter brought a bitter cold snap that hung over the valley. By the end of February, the temperature hovered at twenty below, snow lay frozen on the ground, and driving was treacherous on the mountain curves. The days were short, so it was dark when we sat down for our evening meals.

Late one afternoon I went down to the cellar to get vegetables for supper and noted with dismay how bare the shelves looked. The corn, beans and peas were going fast. And where there should have been tomatoes and pickles was row after row of empty, dusty jars. Going back upstairs, I shook my head as I passed the bag of dill. Then I busied myself at the stove.

Suppertime was my family's favorite time of the day. All fifteen of us sat around a huge oblong table that had been Quincy's mother's. I always spread the table with the prettiest oilcloth I could find. Quincy had made two long padded benches, covered in a cheerful orange, the color of glowing embers. Our oversize kitchen was warm and cozy from the old Monarch wood and coal stove that I cooked on.

We were having a delightful meal, the kids recounting what happened at school, when someone pounded hard on the door. I pushed my chair back, mumbling "Who in the world would be out in this bitter cold—and in the dark too?"

Standing in the entryway was one of our neighbors, a man in his late thirties with a full dark beard that was glazed and white with frost. He looked like Santa Claus.

"Mrs. Huyser," he said as he stepped into the warm kitchen, "how many fresh cucumbers and tomatoes can you use?"

The clatter of knives and forks ceased. All eyes fastened on our bearded visitor. With my mouth agape, I thought, *Did I hear right?* Fresh cucumbers and tomatoes in February? I was speechless.

"I have a two-ton truck outside more than half full with cucumbers, tomatoes, green beans—even eggplant." Quincy and I zipped up our winter jackets, tugged on mittens and trudged out to look.

Our neighbor's teeth were on the verge of chattering, but his soft voice was steady and clear. "The produce was on its way from Mexico, but the road coming down the canyon was so icy that the truck slid into the Gallatin River."

"How come it didn't freeze?" I blurted.

"All the boxes that landed on the bank did freeze, but the ones that went in the river were okay. The insurance company hired me to get the truck out and let me keep whatever I wanted. So I salvaged this stuff." He thumped the side of the truck. "I figured you could use some of this with your big family. The only thing is," he added somewhat apologetically, "my wife will want the green beans since she didn't get to can any last summer."

I managed to say, "That's one thing I *did* can."

We packed in nine big boxes of beautiful Beefsteak-size tomatoes and box after box of firm, green, perfect-for-pickling cucumbers, and the next day I prepared for canning.

I was surprised that some of the dill was still green, and the rest revived in a warm water bath. By early March I had canned ninety-two quarts of ice pickles, bread-and-butter pickles, and, of course, crisp dills. It was the only time I had ever been able to "play" at pickling, not pressured to can everything at once, as I was at harvesttime.

I was putting up the pickles when I remembered what the Lord had said to me seven months before: "Does it really matter if it comes out of *your* garden or not?" and when I answered, "I know it all comes from You," I didn't dream it would come from an ice-cold, fast-flowing mountain river.

But then I don't even *try* to fathom His ways. I simply don't have the imagination.

Chapter 4   Quiet Protection

Anyone who's ever cared for a child knows that most of the time children are totally unaware of the extent of care and protection afforded them. When a toddler barrels across a yard with her eye on her Big Wheel, she is oblivious to the dangers lurking between her and her goal. So her mother chases behind her, swinging her up at the last moment so she doesn't tumble over the rake. How many parents have trotted along beside a novice bicyclist as he learns to ride without training wheels. Even though the attentive adult is outside the child's view, their protection is none the less real and effective.

God protects us with the same care and love. Even when we're not fully aware of it, God's hand lifts us up when we are in danger, snatching us out of harm's way. He keeps His promise: "He will not let your foot slip—he who watches over you will not slumber" (Psalm 121:3). Sometimes it's only in looking back that we can see what God has done. We see the special warnings or the circumstances altered ever so minutely or the call received at just the right moment. God's hand may sometimes be hidden, but it is without doubt at work in our lives.

The LORD is faithful to all his promises
and loving toward all he has made.
The LORD upholds all those who fall
and lifts up all who are bowed down.
The eyes of all look to you,
and you give them their food at the proper time.
You open your hand
and satisfy the desires of every living thing.

—Psalm 145:13–16

MIRACLE OF THE BROKEN ANSWERING MACHINE

BETH REINKE

The shrill ring sounded in my ear for the seventh time. "I guess they don't have an answering machine or it would have picked up by now," I said aloud into the phone receiver. It was the second day I had attempted, unsuccessfully, to RSVP for an in-home demonstration party hosted by my friend Kristin Green.

A few days later, I was standing at the kitchen counter pouring a glass of milk when I suddenly felt an overwhelming urge to call Kristin again. Glancing at the clock, I hesitated, mentally ticking off the list of things I needed to do before ushering my two preschoolers to bed.

Then I remembered what I had been reading during my devotional time. I was working through a study guide on the Holy Spirit written by Charles Stanley. The well-known author/pastor emphasized that being obedient to God meant submitting to the Holy Spirit's sudden promptings of what to do or say.

I quickly punched in Kristin's number. Her husband, Paul, cheerfully answered. I rattled off my message for Kristin. Then I heard myself asking "...and how are *you*, Paul?" even though I didn't know him well.

He laughed as he told me a bee had stung him on the hand earlier that day.

"Ouch!" I said empathetically, cringing inside. Since my family suffered from myriad allergies, bees were among my *least* favorite of God's creatures.

"Are you allergic to bee stings?" I asked, trying to discover why he would bother to mention such a thing.

"No," he said, "but, you know, my tongue is feeling a little funny."

A tingle of fear raced down my spine. I knew some people are extremely allergic to bee stings. The poison can cause their tongue to swell and block their airway, possibly leading to suffocation.

Paul seemed fine on the phone. *His voice is animated and his speech sounds normal, so surely his tongue couldn't be swollen,* I thought. But I drew a shaky breath, and decided to err on the side of safety.

"Paul," I blurted out, "you could be in a life-threatening situation. Do you have any Benadryl in the house?"

He wasn't sure. I instructed him to scour the medicine cabinet and, if he found some, to take a dose immediately. Then I hung up, promising to call back shortly.

Oh, Lord, I prayed, *what should I do for Paul? He's alone with three little boys, and he might be getting sick.* I knew from our conversation that the baby was safe in his crib. But the other two, ages two and three-and-a-half, were not in bed yet.

I contemplated calling 911, explaining that someone ten miles away from me might be having a severe reaction to a bee sting. Instead, I dialed a friend who lived less than a mile from Paul. She could get to him faster than an ambulance, plus she was a registered nurse. But no one answered.

I called Paul back. He had not found any Benadryl. His conversation was quite pleasant and articulate.

I kept asking questions. Finally, Paul admitted that his hand was feeling funny, too. Realizing someone should check on him immediately, I asked Paul for phone numbers of his closest neighbors. He joked about not being good with phone numbers, but was able to give me the first and last names of a few neighbors, even spelling their last names. I hung up and snatched my phone book from the drawer.

I flipped through it as fast as my trembling fingers could turn the pages, looking for numbers. At the first house an answering machine clicked on.

My pulse racing, I scrambled to locate the second number. When a woman answered, her voice was like salve on my anxious heart. I poured out the story, and she agreed to run over to Paul's house right away. *Thank You, Lord*, I prayed silently. *And please let Paul be okay. Those boys need their daddy.*

Just to be sure help had arrived, I called Paul's house again a few minutes later. The neighbor I had contacted was there with another neighbor who was a nurse. The nurse brought some Benadryl from her house and coaxed Paul into swallowing it, while an ambulance was on its way. Less than ten minutes elapsed between the time Paul told me about the bee sting and the time the neighbor administered the Benadryl.

The next morning, Kristin told me the complete story. She and her oldest son came home after his soccer game to find a group of people gathered in the driveway, while neighborhood wives watched the younger boys in the house. After my call, the neighbor had found Paul slumped in an easy chair, too weak to walk or lift his arms, with his face so swollen his eyes were barely visible. His hand was swollen to three times its normal size.

Why hadn't Paul told me how ill he was feeling? I wondered. I apologized for not immediately calling 911 and silently chastised myself for not instantly recognizing the severity of the situation. Kristin assured me Paul had a long-standing habit of downplaying any illness, even when he had a terrible case of the flu.

"I think he's learned his lesson this time," she said with a chuckle. "Luckily he had you for a guardian angel."

"Well, it's a good thing you guys don't have an answering machine," I said, "or I would have just left a message days ago instead of calling last night."

"Oh, we *do* have a machine," Kristin assured me. "But it broke last week."

Their answering machine was broken. I let the fact sink in, then smiled, imagining

God disconnecting the inner workings of the answering machine with a screwdriver. Humbled and grateful, I realized God had used *me* to help save Paul's life.

We have a loving, all-knowing God who puts us in the right place (or dialing the right phone number) at the right time. Sometimes He has to give us a heavenly nudge to accomplish His will.

THE MISSING SHOES

ELIZABETH SHERRILL

O f all times to have the airline lose my luggage! It was only my toiletries case with my one pair of good shoes, but of all places to wind up without them.

I'd flown out to Farmington, New Mexico, for a one-day seminar sponsored by the Southwest Christian Writers' Association. "No one will care about your shoes," Margaret, the group's president, assured me.

Doubtless Margaret was right, but *of all times*. Even as I said it, a phrase came to mind: ". . . we should at all times, and in all places, give thanks unto Thee." At *all* times.

We met at the First Presbyterian Church. At the seminar's close, several writers came up to the speaker's stand. Suddenly there was a terrifying *crack*. Then a woman shouted, "Lie down! Everyone!"

Two men were outside, one of them brandishing a gun. The sound of exploding glass had come from the window. Later we learned that the men had been drinking and shooting at telephone poles. From the wall beyond the speaker's stand, the police recovered the tip of an electric screwdriver fired from a homemade pistol.

While Margaret filled out the police report, the rest of us said good-bye, each no doubt recalling a step forward or a delay that had kept him or her out of the line of fire.

For my part, I was tracing a trajectory, from the window to the wall, an inch over the spot where I'd been standing. I was thinking of a pair of two-and-a-half inch heels in a missing bag, and echoing a prayer: ". . . we should at all times, and in all places, give thanks to Thee, O Lord."

DIAGNOSIS CONFIRMED

JOAN WESTER ANDERSON

Seventh-grader Michael Halas had always enjoyed good health, so when he began running fever after fever, his parents were concerned. Then during one bout, Michael had joint pain as well. His father, John, remembered having read some articles about a newly discovered illness called Lyme disease, which had recently become more prevalent in their Voorhees, New Jersey, community. The symptoms of Lyme disease mimicked many others, including juvenile rheumatoid arthritis, and some patients became very ill or even permanently disabled if the disease was not caught in its early stages. "Could this be Lyme disease?" John Halas asked the pediatrician the next time Michael ran a fever and was taken to the doctor's office.

"Not a chance," she answered without hesitation. "It's just a typical adolescent virus."

The Halas family had great confidence in this doctor, so they hesitated to argue. "But I remember reading something about joint pain being a symptom of Lyme," John persisted.

"It accompanies viruses, too," the doctor assured him. The family went home. On the one hand, they were grateful that the doctor seemed so positive and that

Michael would be spared such a serious sickness. But John had trouble sleeping that night. What if they were all wrong?

A few days later, for reasons now forgotten, Mr. and Mrs. Halas exchanged cars. John traveled over one of the Delaware River bridges into Philadelphia from South Jersey. Returning to Jersey later that afternoon, he suddenly saw a piece of paper fly across the hood of the car and wedge itself somewhere under the edge. "It kept flapping like it was waving to me," John says. He sped up, trying to dislodge it, but with no success. The bothersome item hung on for the next fifteen miles, until John was able to get back to his office, park and get out to see what it was.

The paper was actually a pamphlet of about ten pages, open in the middle, with one half under the rim of the car's hood, wedged so perfectly that it looked as if it had been placed there by hand. Moreover, it was too thick to have stuck under the hood of his own car, had he been driving it that day. John took the pamphlet out, turned it over, and looked at the title. It was a booklet on Lyme disease.

"I ran to my office and read the book from cover to cover," John says. "I then phoned my wife, told her what had happened, and we set off for the doctor's office. I didn't tell the doctor about the booklet then; we just said we wanted a Lyme disease test done ASAP." The doctor agreed, and the family had the results in about three days. The test was positive.

"Michael went on medication for the next thirty days, and the Lyme disease cleared up," John says. "We had caught it in time. Today Michael is healthy, strong and healed."

Was it just a coincidence that the medical knowledge this family needed was provided to them in such a unique way? You decide.

COMING THROUGH IN THE CLUTCH

TOM SHERIDAN

It happened on a trip in our Volkswagen van when my wife and I were newlyweds. During the journey, there was a persistent problem with the van's clutch; the pedal wouldn't come all the way up after being released.

I stopped in a small town long enough to crawl under the van and remove the sheet metal cover from the pedal mechanism. As soon as I did, the clutch pedal popped all the way to its normal position. It seemed, at first, as though there had been some sort of interference from the covering. This was a very strange thing, since mechanical parts generally work in predictable ways. This one didn't.

So I asked my wife to slide over into the driver's seat and step on the clutch as I watched what happened from beneath. As she moved, her foot bumped ever so lightly against the brake. I still remember lying there on my back watching in amazement as the brake pedal—with which we'd had no trouble—fell all the way down to the floorboard. The bolt holding it in place had been hanging on by its last thread. Just the slight bump finished the job.

Certainly, the next time I tried to stop the van it would have failed. We would have been seriously injured, possibly killed.

It was the dropping clutch pedal that led me under the van to check it out—the clutch pedal that "magically" cured itself the moment I looked at it.

I called my wife to look. Together we lay on our backs beneath the van as I explained what had just happened. That moment, more than twenty years ago, is frozen in time for us. It was a miracle moment that served to put our marriage on a different plane, one higher than self.

There never was anything wrong with the clutch. It worked fine for many more years. I have always considered the "miracle of the good clutch and the broken brake" to be my greatest gift. After seeing a miracle right before my eyes, I never again needed faith; I had proof. And when things go wrong, as they sometimes will, I remember that God is watching over me.

A TEXTBOOK EXAMPLE

ROBERTA MESSNER

A gust of ice-cold wind pierced my face as I left the warmth of my classroom and headed across the college campus to the library, my *Medical-Surgical Nursing* textbook in hand. "Are you sure you don't want to go eat lunch with us and study for tomorrow's psychology quiz?" asked one of my fellow classmates. "That neuro exam isn't until next week. We can cram for that later."

I didn't understand it, but I couldn't shake the feeling that I should study the neurology nursing material today. I located a secluded spot in the library, peeled off my heavy wool coat, scarf and gloves, and opened the text to a section of the "Neurological Nursing" chapter we hadn't yet even covered in class: the signs and symptoms of head injury. I found myself totally absorbed in the material, even imagining that I was taking care of such a patient.

I glanced at my watch and was startled to discover it was 6:30 P.M. I hadn't even stopped to eat. I was supposed to pick up my mother and sisters by 7:00 P.M. and drive to church for the midweek prayer service. Pulling into the driveway at home, I honked the horn and sat back to wait. But my family, usually so prompt, did not appear.

When I dashed up to the house to see what was delaying them, I found my mother lying across the porch steps. "I slipped on a little patch of ice, but I'm not hurt," she explained. "I think I just scraped my arm a little."

"Maybe you should go to the emergency room, just to be sure you're okay," I suggested as we helped her back into the house and onto the sofa. One sister brought an ice pack for Mother's arm and another got her a glass of ginger ale.

A short time later, Mother complained of feeling nauseated. "It's probably just the ginger ale; I'm okay, really," she insisted. "Just let me go to sleep." But then we noticed even stranger behavior. One moment she was giggling excitedly, the next she was drowsy, and the next moment, she tried to push us away, which was so unlike Mother. And there was something different about her touch, there was a certain weakness about it.

A detailed list formed in my mind as vividly as the words had appeared earlier in the afternoon on the pages of my nursing textbook. The symptoms of a head injury: nausea . . . alternating levels of consciousness . . . weakness.

I grabbed a flashlight and checked Mother's pupils. They were unequal in size and barely receptive to light. My mother was a textbook example of a patient with a head injury.

We rushed Mother to the hospital, where surgery was performed to remove a blood clot in her brain. After the operation, the neurosurgeon informed our family:

"Your mother is in the intensive care unit and her condition is stable. If she had been permitted to go to bed tonight, it's very likely she would have died in her sleep."

I studied the doctor's knitted brow and grave eyes in astonishment. God had spared my mother's life.

One cold winter afternoon, my classmates had tried to convince me that we had nearly a week to prepare for our neurology nursing examination, but I had been compelled to study the material that day, as if I were actually caring for such a patient. As it turned out, I had done just that.

BROUGHT BACK TO LIFE

KELSEY TYLER

Scarlet fever hit the Bedford home in the spring of 1946. Rosemary and Bill Bedford lived in an old rambling farmhouse on the outskirts of town and the only medical attention they could afford was an occasional house call from the local family doctor.

"Looks like they all have it, even the little one," the doctor said grimly after diagnosing the Bedford's three daughters one morning. "I'll have to put a quarantine on the house and you'll need to care for the girls around the clock. Give them aspirin for the fever and keep them cool with wet rags. I'll check on you again in a few days."

The Bedfords were gravely concerned as the doctor closed the door behind him. Ellie, ten, and Bonnie, six, were old enough to withstand the vicious illness. But little Susie wasn't even three yet and her fever was highest of all.

"I'm not sure what to do," Rosemary admitted tearfully, her voice hushed so the children wouldn't hear her. She looked into her husband's eyes and he saw the fear there. "I'm so afraid, Bill."

Bill placed his large, work-worn hands on her shoulders and did his best to soothe away her tension. "We'll just take it one hour at a time and pray that the girls get better quickly. Lots of people have scarlet fever, Rosemary. Everything'll be all right. You'll see."

The work of caring for three very sick children was overwhelming. They took turns working with each child, attending to their fevers and seeing that they were all drinking enough water.

But as the days wore on, Susie continued to get worse.

"Did you give her aspirin yet?" Bill asked, wearily, finding Rosemary in the kitchen. One week had passed since the doctor's visit, and the older two girls were showing signs of improving. Only Susie remained desperately sick.

"Yes, is she hot again already?"

"Burning up."

Rosemary hung her head and quietly began crying, exhausted and discouraged that nothing seemed to be helping their youngest daughter.

Bill watched her compassionately and checked the clock on the wall. It was nearly eight o'clock.

"Listen, honey, why don't you go on upstairs and get some sleep tonight? I'll stay up with Susie and make sure her fever doesn't get too high."

Rosemary looked up and Bill saw that her eyes were only half-open. She waited a moment, thinking about her options, and finally she nodded. "You'll come get me if anything changes?"

"Yes, don't worry about a thing. I'll give her some more aspirin now and then I'll sit right beside her all night. She'll probably do much better tomorrow."

Rosemary stood up slowly and kissed Bill on the cheek. "Thank you," she whispered. Ten minutes later she was asleep in bed.

Bill tiptoed into Susie's room and found the child curled up in her crib, "Susie," he cooed. "It's Daddy. Daddy's here now. Everything's okay."

He walked up to the wooden railing and felt her skin. It was dry and parched and even hotter than before. A burst of panic surged through him but he forced himself to remain calm. Gently he lifted her into his arms and sat down with her in a nearby rocking chair.

"Wake up, honey, I have some aspirin for you."

The child's eyes fluttered and Bill noticed how cracked her lips were. Her fever was raging and he worried that the heat might be dehydrating her body. He gave her the tiny pink children's aspirin tablets and a sip of water.

"Drink some more, baby," he said in a soothing voice.

"No, Daddy," she cried. "No more."

Then she was asleep again. She lay her head on his shoulder and fell asleep against him. Bill's upper body began to sweat from the intense heat of the child against him.

"Please, God, let her get through this," he whispered. Then he ran his hand gently over her hot forehead and began humming to her.

Hours passed and the aspirin seemed to have no effect on the child's fever. Bill began using wet cloths to cool her body, but still the fever raged.

Sometime after midnight Bill noticed that Susie's breathing had begun to grow more difficult. *How will I know if this is really an emergency?* he asked himself. *At what point do I forget the quarantine and take her to the hospital? Help me, God.*

Then at 4:30 that morning, with everyone else in the house still asleep, Susie made a terrible gasping sound and suddenly bent over backward, contorting her spine so that the back of her head nearly touched her hips.

She made the gasping sound once more and Bill saw that she was arching backward in an attempt to breathe. Her airways seemed to have closed down, making it impossible for her to inhale. He carried her through the house as fast as he could, called the local doctor, and explained the situation.

"You need to get her to the hospital immediately," he said. "I'll call ahead and make arrangements."

The hospital was only six miles away so Bill raced to wake up his wife and daughters and the family drove as fast as they could with Susie in the front seat, still gasping for air.

"Dear God, help us," Rosemary cried, clinging to the girl and rocking her as Bill drove and silently committed Susie's fate to God.

Lord, You know how much I love my girls and You know how special each of them is to me and Rosemary. But things don't look good for Susie right now. I want You to know something. If You take our littlest angel, I'll still trust You. She belongs to You, after all. But oh, Lord, if You'll let us keep her for a while longer, I swear I'll do my very best to raise her right.

The hospital was still two miles away when the Bedfords began to hear a strange gurgling in Susie's throat. About the same time, she stopped trying to gasp for air and her lips began to turn blue.

"Bill!" Rosemary shouted. "She's not breathing." She shook the small child firmly. "Susie! Wake up, come on, honey. Breathe, Susie! Please breathe."

Bill raced around another corner and whipped the car into the hospital parking lot. He had barely stopped the car when Rosemary rushed from the passenger seat, carrying Susie in her arms, and ran into the emergency room.

The nurses were waiting and one of them took Susie from her mother and lay her on an examining table. "This child's dead," she shouted. "Someone get the doctor."

Rosemary screamed in her grief and watched in horror as the nurse tried in vain to find Susie's pulse. At that instant, a young intern came racing down the hallway and moved the nurse aside. He massaged Susie's chest and then listened to her heart.

"Nothing," he murmured. Then he repeated the procedure two times until finally he heard a heartbeat.

Without waiting he swept her into his arms and carried her into a room where he hooked her up to forced oxygen. For the next several hours he worked over her without stopping while her parents and sisters waited in the hallway.

Finally, the exhausted intern approached the Bedfords and slipped his hands into the pockets of his white jacket. "She's breathing on her own now," he said, offering only a hint of a sad smile. "But she has slipped into a coma. There is no telling how long before she'll come out of it. Or even if she'll come out."

Relief mixed with uncertainty flooded the faces of Bill and Rosemary. Bill stepped forward and shook the young doctor's hand. "The nurse said she was dead, Doctor. What happened?"

The intern nodded. "Technically, she had already died when your wife brought her in. She wasn't breathing and had no heartbeat. But I knew she was probably suffering from scarlet fever and that meant you'd probably been giving her baby aspirin to bring down her fever."

Bill nodded. "She's had it several times today, since her fever just kept rising. Every four hours just like the bottle says."

"That's what I suspected. You see, we're just learning about aspirin poisoning, Mr. Bedford. I've been doing research on it for the past year and I recognized her symptoms as being identical to what we will one day expect to see in a case of aspirin poisoning."

"Aspirin poisoning?" Rosemary looked confused. "But aspirin is the only thing that helps a child with scarlet fever. And we never gave her more than the correct dose for her age."

The intern nodded. "Normally there wouldn't be a problem, Mrs. Bedford. But sometimes a child will have a reaction, possibly when there is too much aspirin accumulated in her body, and then her fever will climb even higher."

He explained that as the fever increases, septicemia sets in—infection throughout the body. After that, the respiratory system can shut down under the strain and the patient can die.

"Is it common, Doctor?" Bill asked. "I've never heard anything about this in the past."

The intern raised an eyebrow and shook his head. "That's the amazing thing, Mr. Bedford. There hasn't been a single documented case of aspirin poisoning yet. Just speculation and research."

"But if you hadn't known what to look for . . ." Bill stopped in mid-sentence.

"She wouldn't have made it," the intern said quietly. "Thank God I was here tonight and I knew what to look for." He paused a moment and stared intently at the couple. "Normally I would have gone home hours ago but just after midnight something told me to stay a little later and work on my patient charts. Strange how things work, isn't it?"

He turned then and went back to check on Susie while Rosemary and Bill stared at each other in disbelief. Bill felt his eyes well up with tears and he struggled to speak.

"I asked the Lord to spare our little Susie tonight," he said, his chin quivering. "But I told Him if He wanted to take Susie home I would let her go. It's a miracle, Rosemary, but tonight He brought her back to life so she could spend a little more time with us."

Rosemary nodded and collapsed against her husband, tears spilling onto her cheeks. Nearby, the older girls, too, were crying. "I thought we'd lost her, Bill," Rosemary whispered.

"God knows what He's doing, honey. You watch," he pulled away so he could see his wife's eyes. "She'll come out of that coma and she'll be just fine."

In the days that followed, Rosemary and Bill and another couple who were close friends of the Bedford family took turns sitting with Susie and praying for her. On the tenth morning, the Bedfords received a telephone call early in the morning. It was Susie's nurse at the hospital.

"Come down quickly," she said and Bill could hear the smile in her voice. "Susie's awake and she's asking for you."

"Is she all right?" Bill sat up in bed and waited breathlessly for the answer.

"Yes, Mr. Bedford. She's fine. But she'll be a lot happier when she can see her mommy and daddy."

Today, the miracle of what happened to Susie Bedford lives on. Her case is documented in the files at Children's Hospital in Denver as the first official incident of aspirin poisoning. Doctors still are not sure what the young intern did that night to save the child from advanced respiratory failure.

As for the Bedfords, Bill and Rosemary watched Susie grow into a beautiful young woman whose faith was every bit as strong as theirs. They remain thankful for her life, much as they were that dreadful night. And several times a year they send a donation to Children's Hospital in remembrance of a certain young intern who was placed in their path one freezing night in 1946 by way of a miracle.

THE BULLET

DORIS SANFORD

t was a late March afternoon and Anya sat in the car memorizing Bible verses. She did it every week while her little brother, Zeek, had his piano lesson. Her turn would come next, but memorizing meant repeating the verses out loud and that worked best in the car. She was a part of her junior high Bible Quiz team and that required knowing a part of one of the books of the Bible *very* well. No problem. Anya loved the competition!

Their music teacher lived in a two-story house and the piano was upstairs. Just before the lesson began, Zeek told his mom, "I want Sissy to listen to my lesson." Mom reminded him that Anya needed the study time, and besides, she had been listening to him practice his piano lesson all week at home. But Zeek was determined, he went down to the car and to Mom's surprise returned with his big sister in tow.

The lesson began. Five minutes later the lesson was abruptly halted by a loud noise outside. Everyone stopped to watch a late-model car speeding away. The lesson resumed after the teacher reassured them that it was probably the car's backfire they had heard.

Zeek's hands were barely on the piano when the teacher's husband rushed in: "A gun shot . . . into the car . . . shattered the passenger side window in the front seat!"

The lesson was over. They hurried down to look. Sure enough, there was the bullet lodged in the back rest just where Anya's head had been five minutes earlier.

They all knew it immediately. God had used seven-year-old Zeek to save his sister's life. It was a profound moment. Zeek had responded when it hadn't made sense to him or anyone else, and Anya had complied with his illogical request.

The two snipers who were driving through the streets of Salem, Oregon, randomly shooting at mailboxes, cars, and houses were arrested and held on a one-million dollar bail. The district attorney asked Anya and Zeek to come to court and tell their story. The young men were sent to prison for five years, but not without hearing how God had protected a seven-year-old and his big sister.

WHEN THE LIGHTS CAME ON

FRANKLIN GRAHAM

In 1971, as a newly licensed pilot, I was flying with my flight instructor from Vero Beach, Florida, to Longview, Texas. That night, we hit bad weather over Mobile, Alabama, and air-traffic controllers suggested we fly north toward Jackson, Mississippi, to avoid an approaching storm.

As we rose above the clouds, I noticed the instrument panel lights flicker. A minute later, radios and instruments started going dead, then all our lights went out. Our situation was desperate, and as we flew an emergency triangle, we prayed to God for His protection. We decided to drop below the clouds and try to see the ground. Soon we spotted the distant lights of Jackson and headed for the airport's rotating beacon.

We circled the control tower twice, then got a green light to land. Without any electric power, we had to lower the landing gear manually. At that moment, all the strobe landing lights came on and slowly, safely we touched ground

Then the landing lights went off. *That's odd*, I thought, *at least they could have waited until we taxied to the ramp*. It was even odder when a man from the tower asked us, "Who gave you permission to land?"

And then, little by little, we learned that no one in the tower had seen us circling overhead. The green light had been flashed by a traffic controller who was explaining to his visiting pastor what he would do in case a plane ever attempted to land without radio communication. The emergency landing lights were part of the same demonstration.

But the whole story can never be explained—just accepted with gratitude, as I strive to serve the Lord each new day.

Chapter 5   Sweet Reunions

Most reunions are planned events. Families have reunions every summer, high school and college classes have reunions every five years, even military veterans meet at regular planned intervals. But probably the sweetest and most precious reunions are those arranged by God.

Most of us have had the experience of losing touch with someone you love, someone who has been a vital part of your life. Sometimes we're separated by uncontrollable circumstances, like war; other times we're separated by more everyday situations like illness or family difficulties. Whatever the circumstances, when we find ourselves separated from those who have touched our lives, brought us love or perhaps even saved our lives, we carry within us an emptiness. We do manage to work around the loss, even though it is never truly healed, but our prayers are always for a reuniting.

There comes a point when all our own efforts to find this person fail: telephone directories, Internet searches, alumni lists, veterans administration, old friends, former neighbors. Nothing works and no one can help. And that's when God works one of His miracles, bringing into our lives once again the people we thought were lost forever, in a reunion that is certainly beyond coincidence.

"For I know the plans I have for you," declares the LORD, "plans to prosper you and not to harm you, plans to give you hope and a future. Then you will call upon me and come and pray to me, and I will listen to you. You will seek me and find me when you seek me with all your heart. I will be found by you," declares the LORD, "and will bring you back from captivity...."

—Jeremiah 29:11–14

WAITING TO GO HOME

Veronica Kelly

An elderly couple came to our animal shelter. They were very hesitant in their manner and spent a lot of time getting to the point of their visit.

"Maybe we had better go ahead and tell them that our daughter was in an accident and died and maybe they will understand," the wife said. They proceeded to say that their daughter had had a cat, but since her death, the cat refused to settle into their home without her there. They wanted to know if Mother Superior would take this huge orange tabby cat. They said they did not know how old it was and signed it in.

Our shelter has a no-kill policy. Unwanted cats and dogs either wait to be adopted out, or they live the rest of their lives in a kennel environment.

After the couple left, Mother Superior called down to the cat building and asked one of the Sisters to come and get the cat. Our Irish Sister Mary Brenda came up to carry the orange fur ball to his new home.

Usually, a new arrival is placed in a small cage or run for twenty-four hours so it can adjust to its new environment and the free-roving pets. But, as Sister Brenda carried the newly abandoned cat into the room, it jumped out of her arms, leapt up onto a window ledge, and sat there, looking down the long driveway.

From that moment on, the cat stayed in that spot all the time. No one ever saw it leave its perch to go outside. Only Sister Mary Brenda, who had such a gentle way with all the cats, could go near it.

In the next six years we moved the shelter three times and took the cat, which Sister Mary Brenda nicknamed Kitty, with us each time. We always relocated the catteries near the entrance to the driveways. Once we moved the cats in, Kitty would take his usual place on the window ledge and would resume looking down the driveway. No one wanted to adopt Kitty, because he would not let anyone touch him.

Finally, we moved to a wonderful wooded property. During the day, the cats wandered outside onto fifty-six acres and came in to eat at night. But Kitty always stayed seated on the windowsill looking down the driveway.

One day, as Mother Superior looked out of the office window, a car pulled up the drive. After a while, she saw the car door open. Slowly, crutches emerged, one at a time, as the woman holding them carefully ventured out of the car taking great care with each movement. The woman moved slowly up the stairs to the office.

"I missed my cat over the years and have heard good news about your shelter," the woman said. "I've come to see if I can adopt a cat."

She had been in a car accident a few years before and had been in and out of the hospital all this time, with many surgeries, and now the doctors couldn't do anything more for her. She wanted a cat to replace the one she had loved so much before the accident. Her parents had told her that her much-loved pet had died while she was undergoing surgery.

The two women walked slowly toward the shelter. As Mother Superior opened the door, the woman with crutches started to step up. Suddenly Kitty jumped from his perch on the windowsill and pounced on the woman. She dropped her crutches and fell to the floor, lying on her back. The orange cat—the same cat she had loved so much before her accident—was on her chest. She hugged it for dear life as her cat loved her back for dear life. There was no doubt who the cat had been waiting for.

The woman never did adopt a new cat—she took her own beloved pet home with her. Now our windowsill was free for another cat.

IT HAPPENED ON THE BROOKLYN SUBWAY

PAUL DEUTSCHMAN

The car was crowded, and there seemed to be no chance of a seat. But as I entered, a man sitting by the door suddenly jumped up to leave, and I slipped into the empty seat.

I've been living in New York long enough not to start conversations with strangers. But, being a photographer, I have the peculiar habit of analyzing people's faces, and I was struck by the features of the passenger on my left. He was probably in his late thirties, and when he glanced up, his eyes seemed to have a hurt expression in them. He was reading a Hungarian-language newspaper, and something prompted me to say in Hungarian, "I hope you don't mind if I glance at your paper."

The man seemed surprised to be addressed in his native language. But he only answered politely, "You may read it now. I'll have time later on."

During the half-hour ride to town, we had quite a conversation. He said his name was Bela Paskin. A law student when World War II started, he had been put into a German labor battalion and sent to the Ukraine. Later he was captured by the Russians and put to work burying the German dead. After the war, he covered hundreds of miles on foot until he reached his home in Debrecen, a large city in eastern Hungary.

I myself knew Debrecen quite well, and we talked about it for a while. Then he told me the rest of his story. When he went to the apartment once occupied by his father, mother, brothers and sisters, he found strangers living there. Then he went upstairs to the apartment that he and his wife once had. It also was occupied by strangers. None of them had ever heard of his family.

As he was leaving, full of sadness, a boy ran after him, calling, *"Paskin bacsi! Paskin bacsi!"* That means "Uncle Paskin." The child was the son of some old neighbors of his. He went to the boy's home and talked to his parents. "Your whole family is dead," they told him. "The Nazis took them and your wife to Auschwitz."

Auschwitz was one of the worst Nazi concentration camps. Paskin gave up all hope. A few days later, too heartsick to remain any longer in Hungary, he set out on foot again, stealing across border after border until he reached Paris. He managed to emigrate to the United States in October 1947, just three months before I met him.

All the time he had been talking, I kept thinking that somehow his story seemed familiar. A young woman whom I met recently at the home of friends had also been from Debrecen; she had been sent to Auschwitz; from there she had been transferred to work in a German munitions factory. Her relatives had been killed in the gas chambers. Later, she was liberated by the Americans and was brought here in the first boatload of displaced persons in 1946.

Her story had moved me so much that I had written down her address and phone number, intending to invite her to meet my family and thus help relieve the terrible emptiness in her life.

It seemed impossible that there could by any connection between these two people, but as I neared my station, I fumbled anxiously in my address book. I asked in what I hoped was a casual voice, "Was your wife's name Marya?"

He turned pale. "Yes!" he answered. "How did you know?"

He looked as if he were about to faint.

I said, "Let's get off the train." I took him by the arm at the next station and led him to a phone booth. He stood there like a man in a trance while I dialed her phone number.

It seemed hours before Marya Paskin answered. (Later I learned her room was alongside the telephone, but she was in the habit of never answering it because she had so few friends and the calls were always for someone else. This time, however, there was no one else at home, and after letting it ring for a while, she responded.)

When I heard her voice at last, I told her who I was and asked her to describe her husband. She seemed surprised at the question, but gave me a description. Then I asked her where she had lived in Debrecen, and she told me the address.

Asking her to hold the line, I turned to Paskin and said, "Did you and your wife live on such-and-such a street?"

"Yes!" Bela exclaimed. He was white as a sheet and trembling.

"Try to be calm," I urged him. "Something miraculous is about to happen to you. Here, take this telephone and talk to your wife!"

He nodded his head in mute bewilderment, his eyes bright with tears. He took the receiver, listened a moment to his wife's voice, then suddenly cried, "This is Bela! This is Bela!" and began to mumble hysterically. Seeing that the poor fellow was so excited he couldn't talk coherently, I took the receiver from his shaking hands.

"Stay where you are," I told Marya, who also sounded hysterical. "I am sending your husband to you. We will be there in a few minutes."

Bela was crying like a baby and saying over and over again, "It is my wife. I go to my wife!"

At first I thought I had better accompany Paskin, lest the man should faint from excitement, but I decided that this was a moment in which no strangers should intrude. Putting Paskin into a taxi, I directed the driver to take him to Marya's address, paid the fare and said good-bye.

Bela Paskin's reunion with his wife was a moment so poignant, so electric with suddenly released emotion, that afterward neither he nor Marya could recall much about it.

"I remember only that when I left the phone, I walked to the mirror like in a dream to see if maybe my hair had turned gray," she said later. "The next thing I know, a taxi stops in front of the house, and it is my husband who comes toward me. Details I cannot remember; only this I know—that I was happy for the first time in many years. . . .

"Even now it is difficult to believe that it happened. We have both suffered so much; I have almost lost the capability not to be afraid. Each time my husband goes from the house, I say to myself, 'Will anything happen to take him from me again?'"

Her husband is confident that no horrible misfortune will ever befall them. "Providence has brought us together," he says simply. "It was meant to be."

MOTHER AND CHILD REUNION

CAROLYN CAMPBELL

Until this past April, Kellie Forbes and Shauna Bradley had never met or spoken to each other. Their husbands worked at different companies, their children went to different schools. Now, as Kellie and Shauna prepare to celebrate their first Christmas together, their only regret is that they didn't meet sooner. For more than fourteen years, these two women from Utah unknowingly shared a connection as close as blood; yet only through the most unlikely of circumstances did they find out exactly what it was. Call it chance, call it fate—or call it, if you prefer, a miracle.

In 1992, life looked bleak for Kellie, with three deaths in her family. Then just after moving to a new home, she and her husband were laid off from work. The accumulated problems left her feeling overwhelmed and depressed.

Her company offered layoff counseling with psychotherapist Shauna Bradley. Shauna couldn't help noticing that her client bore an amazing resemblance to her son, Jake, who she had adopted as an infant. She thought that Kellie's dimples, freckles, dark hair and hazel eyes looked exactly like Jake's. But she passed it off as an odd similarity.

During their second session, Shauna asked Kellie about future plans. Kellie said,

"I want to write a book about my adoption experience." As a teenager, she told Shauna, she gave up a baby boy to a couple she never met. Kellie went on to a happy marriage and three other children, but she never stopped thinking about that first son, who would soon celebrate his fourteenth birthday. She hoped that writing about her experience might help other young women.

Kellie's attitude impressed Shauna. She knew she'd be happy to meet her own son's birth mother if she were like Kellie. She told Kellie that as an adoptive mother, this subject was close to her heart.

Grateful to have found a compassionate listener, Kellie tearfully spoke of her one regret: She had not been allowed to hold her son before surrendering him. When asked why, she replied, "Kanab is a small town, and that's just how they did things," referring to the town hundreds of miles away where she'd grown up.

Startled, Shauna dropped her notebook. Her son had been born in Kanab fourteen summers ago. "Did you say Kanab?" she cried. Cautiously, Kellie replied yes.

Suddenly, Shauna felt like she couldn't breathe, as if someone had hit her in the stomach. Then she started hyperventilating. She shook, trembling hands covering her mouth as she repeated, "Oh, my gosh! Oh, my gosh!"

Kellie's words emerged slowly. "Do you have him?"

Shauna nodded, "I think I do."

Taking turns, they shared their stories with each other. As a teenager, Kellie felt ridiculed by classmates in her small-town school. She told Shauna, "I allowed myself to have a physical relationship because I wanted so badly to be accepted."

The result was an unexpected pregnancy when Kellie was eighteen. She broke up with her boyfriend soon after the pregnancy was confirmed and decided to place the baby up for adoption. When her child's future parents were selected, all Kellie was told was their ages, descriptions, and religious and educational backgrounds.

Jim and Shauna Bradley were marred for four years when they applied for adoption after "a lot of infertility work." A year later, they were selected to be parents of a baby from Kanab. Three days after his birth, Jake was presented to the Bradleys. The Bradleys told Jake about his adoption as soon as he could understand, emphasizing that his birth mother gave him up because she loved him. On his birthday, Shauna would say, "You know who's thinking about you today."

Standing in the counselor's office, Kellie didn't know whether to rejoice or be wary. After all she'd endured in the past year, she felt she couldn't risk another bitter disappointment if this woman wasn't her son's mother.

Kellie began, "So his birthday is . . ."

"June twenty, nineteen eighty."

"And the attorney was . . ."

"Mike Mcguire," said Shauna." And wasn't your maiden name Robinson?"

Her heart pounding, Kellie nodded yes. The impossible had happened.

"The odds that we would meet like this do not exist," says Shauna. The two women talked long after the appointment ended. Shauna told Kellie that she wanted to wait until Jake was eighteen to tell him about her, feeling he would be better able to handle the news as an adult. Kellie, happy in the knowledge that her son had a loving home, agreed.

That evening, Jim Bradley could tell that his wife was excited, as if she'd had the best workday ever. After their children were asleep, he found out why Shauna was so overjoyed and shared her excitement.

In the days that followed, Kellie and husband, Thayne, on a counselor's advice, decided to tell their children about the amazing meeting. Their children already knew they had a half-brother who had been given up for adoption to another family. They excitedly asked when they would be meeting Jake.

In the meantime, the Bradleys experienced their own dilemma. Weighing options, they concluded Jake was old enough to be told now. They felt if they waited and he found out they already knew—or if someone else told him—he'd possibly lose trust in them. But if they told him, he could grow into the knowledge of who his birth mother was, and they would be there for him.

When Kellie heard that the Bradleys now wanted to tell Jake as soon as possible, it was her turn to be anxious. "Please don't tell him because you think I want you to," she urged. Now she felt apprehensive. What if she didn't meet Jake's expectations?

One morning, Shauna and Jim came into Jake's room and woke him up. Shauna said, "Jake, the weirdest thing happened. I was counseling with a woman and we realized that she's your birth mother."

Jake burst into a grin. He asked, "What does she look like? When do I get to meet her?" His mother gave him a picture of Kellie. Thrilled, the teen ran off to show the photo to his grandmother.

When Shauna called to say, "We've told him. Can we meet for dinner?" Kellie promptly said yes, thinking: "I'd stop my life for this."

Kellie was first to arrive at the restaurant, and tried to keep her emotions under control. Jim, driving straight from work, was next. Then Shauna drove into the parking lot with Jake. She hadn't even parked the car before Jake jumped out and handed Kellie a beautiful violet.

Kellie's voice quavered, "I've got to give you a hug—I've waited so long for this." As they embraced, Jake's eyes filled with tears and he turned back toward his mother. Shauna comforted him. "It's okay to be emotional, honey. This is a big deal!"

In the restaurant, an excited Jake told Kellie about his hobbies and activities. He was happy that his biological mother shared his love for music, and that his talent for fixing things came from Kellie's father, a mechanic.

Both birth mother and son wept as Kellie said the words she'd always longed to tell him. "There were so many things I knew I couldn't do for you. I wanted you to have a home with a mom and dad. Although I knew I was doing the right thing by giving you up, it was really, really hard."

After their first successful meeting, Shauna and Kellie brought their children together. "Our kids acted as if they'd known each other for a long time," says Kellie.

Today, Kellie and Shauna talk regularly, still amazed at the astonishing coincidence that brought them together. "I'm so happy for Jake," says Shauna. "A piece of his life puzzle has been solved." Adds Kellie, "I'm thrilled Jake has the family he does—they've far exceeded my expectations."

"PAPA!"

GIL SANCHEZ

In the eight months I have lived in Mexico, I've learned a lot about judging people's true character. In the small town of Anhuac where my wife and I run an orphanage, most of the people are very poor, and you have to look past their worn clothes and simple houses to see the richness of their souls. Mostly, I have learned to look at their eyes.

Becky and I had come to do some work at this orphanage several times over the last few years through the sponsorship of our church. After realizing how much help the people needed and after seeing how desperately poor they were, we decided to make our contribution more permanent and committed to a five-year stay. We had two wonderful grown daughters and I had been blessed with much success in my career, so we felt it was time to give back a portion of the many blessings we had received in life. We had no idea that our experience in Mexico would prove to be much more of a renewal of our souls than a sacrifice.

The orphanage is called Casa de la Esperanza, which means House of Hope. For the fifty or so children who live here, it is exactly that. These children have nothing; many have been abandoned by their parents and have lived in unimaginable conditions for many years. But even with their poverty and their past, most of them have a light in their eyes that speaks of faith and hope for a brighter future.

It was at Christmastime here that I really recognized that light among so many. I've enjoyed many wonderful holidays over the years in the luxury and comfort of home in the United States. Surrounded by family and friends, I have celebrated the season with all the normal festivity and tradition—the lights, the music, the shopping, the parties, the tinsel and ornaments—that most American families take for granted. And I have enjoyed the gifts of the season—the new clothes, electronic gadgets, luxuries and toys—given lovingly on those special occasions. But never before have I felt the depth of love that I felt in the midst of these humble children—who had nothing to give—on my first Christmas at the orphanage.

The night of our celebration, all the children were dressed in—what to them was—their Sunday best. They had prepared special decorations and had helped set the table carefully. As a special treat we had turkey for dinner that night, and a savory aroma filled the air. After we ate, everyone joined in singing Christmas carols. There was a small tree in one corner of the room and underneath it, a simple shoebox for each child. The moment they all waited for when each of their names would be called and they would come up and receive their shoebox, had finally arrived.

The first child to be called was Oscar, a small and shy five-year-old, who jumped to his feet at the sound of his name. With both hands in his pockets and a sheepish look of anticipation on his face, he slowly crossed the large floor to receive his gift. The room became silent as everyone's attention focused on him. Suddenly, when he had gone halfway across the room, there was the sound of clapping. As if paying tribute to a king, one little girl started clapping for Oscar as he approached his Christmas shoebox. One by one, others joined in until the whole room was applauding for him. And so it went for each child whose name was called—clapping and more clapping. The children simply couldn't contain their happiness for each other.

In the days following our Christmas party I noticed something different about the way these children played with their gifts compared with what I had observed among American children. Although each child had received just a small box of candies and little plastic toys, they were happy to share whatever they had with each other. I never heard complaints of "that's mine" or "give it back." In fact, after the initial excitement of opening the boxes, no one even seemed aware of what belonged to whom. The joy of simply having received a gift spilled over and created a very generous attitude of "what's mine is yours."

But in fact, it was shortly before Christmas that I really became aware of the good hearts of these people. It was then that I met the seventy-six-year-old man, José Enriquez, or "Papa." I had received a call from someone at the Mexican Department of Social Services (or DIF, as they call it) asking whether we could take in a little

Indian girl who had been found in the streets near the town square. No one knew her name, her age or where she was from, because they couldn't understand the Indian dialect she spoke. We agreed to take her. Upon arriving at the DIF offices to pick her up, I saw a little girl sitting in a chair, legs and arms crossed, clutching a tiny rag doll in her hands. It was obvious that she had been living in the streets for many days. Her face was dirty, her dress was soiled and faded, and she wore only one sock. And on her face—in her wide brown eyes—was an expression of horror.

Behind her frightened stare, though, was a beautiful child. With stone-black hair, almond eyes, and dimpled, chubby cheeks, she was truly one of God's lovely creations. When we attempted to take her back to the orphanage, she cried hysterically; obviously, her recent experience had taught her to trust no one. She had been found by police officials wandering in the town plaza, hungry and somewhat dazed. We learned later that her mother was dead and she had never known her father.

By the end of the first day with us she settled down a bit, finally trusting that no one was going to hurt her. We made up a bed for her, and by nighttime, she had relaxed and was playing with some of the other children, although she still appeared to be on guard and somewhat bewildered. Because the Indian people in this area lived in such squalor, our humble Casa must have seemed like a palace to her, and she took in all the surroundings at the orphanage with a sense of awe.

Two days passed and little Angelica (which we had learned was her name) was beginning to warm up to us. On the third day, around five o'clock in the afternoon, we had a visitor. An old, weary man walked up to the orphanage. Too thin from lack of food and appearing as if he had been wearing the same clothes for weeks, his dark, lined face and leathery hands told of a hard lifetime of working in the sun. He was hunched over and wore an old straw cowboy hat. I thought he was just another villager looking for work—yard work, perhaps—and I would have to tell him that all the positions at the Casa had been filled. But as he approached, something drew me to him.

It was his eyes. They were kind and loving and there was just a spark of hope left in them, though I could tell his life had given him every reason to be cold and bitter. His dialect was unfamiliar to me but his eyes told me had come to the orphanage seeking something far more important than a job. He held out a worn piece of paper, trying to explain something to me that I couldn't understand. When he insisted that I look at the piece of paper, I realized it was a picture of someone, although it was obviously a third- or fourth- generation photocopy and the image was difficult to make out.

Then I saw it. The hope in his eyes and the pleading in his voice were suddenly clear to me. The picture was of Angelica. She was his beloved five-year-old granddaughter. He had been searching for three weeks, posting these flyers with her picture in every town between here and his home of Chihuahua, ninety miles away.

My heart skipped a beat as I thought about the miracle of his finding her. What if he had come here earlier in his search, before Angelica's arrival, and we had sent him on his way? Angelica had been with us only two days, but she had been missing for three weeks! What if Papa had given up what seemed like a fruitless search in a country that contains millions of poverty-stricken children?

Over the next few hours Papa shared his story with us. He had walked for fifteen days though the crowded streets of his city of a half-million people, returning home each night, worried and heart-broken. He later explained that he couldn't even bring himself to turn on the lights at home each night because he would see his grand-daughter's belongings throughout the house. He continued on to Cuauhternoc, a city of one hundred and fifty thousand people, and, after several days of searching there, walked twelve more miles to Anhuac. Now, after twenty-one weary days of searching, he had ended up at the orphanage.

With the last of his money spent on making photocopies of the flyer, the old Taramara Indian man hadn't eaten in days, and had only slept when he could, along the streets of each city. I would later learn that this kind man had taken in a hungry teenager some months before, but returned from work one evening to find both the teenager and Angelica gone. Many young children in Mexico are sold through a black market, and this was probably the teenager's intent with Angelica, but somehow this little girl had managed to escape.

After it dawned on me that the girl in the picture was really Angelica, I looked up at him and smiled. I slowly nodded my head yes and saw his discouraged expression change and his eyes light up with surprise and joy. We walked down the hall together, and I left him there with my wife while I went to find Angelica. He must not have heard her coming, but when he turned around and saw his little granddaughter, he slowly reached up with one hand to remove his hat while the other hand covered his eyes to hide his tears. He struggled to kneel so he could embrace her as everyone stood and watched this joyous reunion. "Papa! Papa!" Angelica cried as she ran the short distance into his arms. They didn't speak, but just held each other and sobbed. And so did we.

As José and Angelica ate dinner with us that night, I looked down to see them holding hands under the table. They hardly took their eyes off each other, needing reassurance that they indeed had been reunited and that their frightening journey had finally ended.

They would return to their village the next day, but I knew in my heart that the image of this man and his angelic granddaughter would be with me forever. As I pictured José walking day after day, week after week, through the dry dusty streets of each city, I realized I was sitting next to a man who understood the meaning of devotion in its purest sense. As I thought of him trudging along without food in his stomach, money in his pocket, or a change of clothes on his back, with hope as his only guide, I no longer worried about the care Angelica would receive during the rest of her childhood. Her Papa had not let her down, and I knew he would love her as no one else could as long as he lived. After all, I had seen it in his eyes.

A BROKEN TAILLIGHT

KELSEY TYLER

There is a story about the highway patrol officer who tentatively pulls over an eighteen-wheeler on a dark, deserted highway. As he approaches the cab, he realizes he has not radioed for backup and he hopes there will be no confrontation.

"Got a light out, back of the truck, left side," the officer states, noting that the trucker is a thousand miles from his home base. "No ticket this time. Just get it fixed."

The trucker's eyes narrow and he climbs down from the cab, staring strangely at the officer. "What'd you say?"

The officer shifts his weight uncomfortably and repeats himself.

The trucker is silent several seconds. Then he speaks. "You were in Vietnam, weren't you?" he asks, his eyes narrow, searching those of the officer.

"Yes." The officer is puzzled. "Why?"

Drifting back in time, the trucker narrates the incident clearly. His military unit was under heavy attack and he had been hit badly. The others were about to flee in a waiting helicopter and had wanted to leave him behind. But the commanding officer would not allow it. He worked over the bleeding soldier until he could be transferred to a gurney and lifted into the helicopter.

"I couldn't see you very well," the trucker says. "But I forced myself to remember your voice so that someday I could find you and thank you. I've prayed about this meeting every day since then. I begged God to let me meet you. You saved my life, and I couldn't imagine leaving this life without the chance to tell you thanks."

The trucker prays for the chance to thank the man who once saved his life. He's a thousand miles away from home when he's pulled over by the very man who rescued him—all because a taillight was out.

Answered prayer? Can it be that God is listening if only we will ask?

Chapter 6　Full Circle

Sometimes it takes years to resolve a situation. In Genesis, we read the story of Joseph, who was sold into slavery by his brothers, and believed he would never see them or his father again. But years later, after being rescued from slavery and then from prison, Joseph became a high official in Egypt and was placed in charge of food resources. Famine struck the land, and guess who showed up to get food for their families? That's right, Joseph's brothers. Eventually, Joseph settled his entire family in Egypt, with the profound awareness of God's hand both in their separation and their reunion. He forgave them their past mistreatment saying, "But God sent me ahead of you to preserve for you a remnant on earth and to save your lives by a great deliverance. So then, it was not you who sent me here, but God" (Genesis 45:7–8). He not only forgave them, he showed his brothers how God could even use their ill behavior to save the entire family.

Joseph understood that none of the events in his life were the result of accident or God's abandonment, and that the reappearance of his brothers was not a "coincidence." It was God's provision to protect Jacob's family.

It may take years to catch a glimpse of what God may be doing. Sometimes it's simply a matter of relying on faith and obedience. But when we face difficulties that we cannot understand, we can be sure God's faithfulness will bring the story full circle.

I will remember the deeds of the LORD;
yes, I will remember your miracles of long ago.
I will meditate on all your works
and consider all your mighty deeds.
Your ways, O God, are holy.
What god is so great as our God?
You are the God who performs miracles;
you display your power among the peoples.

—Psalm 77:11–14

THE MYSTERY RING

AUTHOR UNKNOWN

My husband and I couldn't have been happier when our youngest son Will, then a senior at Yale Law School, announced that he wanted to ask his college girlfriend Jillian to marry him. We'd met Jillian briefly on a couple of occasions, and she appeared to be a lovely young woman.

Will, ever the romantic, informed us that he'd already asked Jillian's father for permission to marry his daughter. And now he wanted us to plan every detail of his proposal.

"I want this to be a big surprise," he said. "And I want her family there. Do you think Jillian's parents as well as her grandparents could join us at Christmas? She's an only child, and her family is really close."

My husband and I told Will we'd love to have them. As we chatted about the arrangements, I asked Will, "What are you going to do for a ring?"

"I wanted to talk to you about that, Mom. Jillian is an old-fashioned girl, and she loves antique jewelry. Does Grandma Margaret have any beautiful old rings she would spare?"

"Oh, honey," I said. "You know that Grandmother already gave her wedding ring to your brother when he got married."

"But perhaps she has some other family jewelry?" he asked.

"I'm not sure," I said, "but I'll ask her."

The truth was, I knew my mother had a ring set with a beautiful emerald that would be perfect. As a little girl I'd admired it whenever I snuck a peek into my mother's jewelry box. But I'd never seen my mother wear this ring. And once, when I'd asked her if I could borrow it for a special occasion, she'd curtly denied the request and refused to explain.

I was hesitant to broach the subject again, but for Will's sake, I decided it was worth the risk. The next day I phoned her and told her of Will's plans. Then I asked, "Do you still have that emerald ring you kept in your jewelry box all those years?"

"I don't think that will work," she said briskly. "He'll just have to buy her a ring."

It was clear by her tone that this was the end of the discussion. But I was now more curious than ever about the emerald ring.

The next day my mother came for supper. I was more than a little surprised when I saw her quietly place a blue velvet box in front of Will's plate. "Here's an engagement ring for Jillian," she announced quietly to her grandson.

When Will opened the box, there lay the antique emerald ring. He was beside himself with gratitude and excitement. "Thank you, Grandma Margaret! Jillian's going to love this ring. Did grandfather give it to you?"

My mother ignored his question and said simply, "I hope your bride will enjoy it."

I spent the next few weeks decorating the house for Christmas. I wanted the holidays to be perfect for Will's engagement. He called numerous times from college, making sure I'd taken care of details, especially the Christmas angel.

It was our family's tradition to put the angel on the tree after dinner on Christmas Eve. As part of our little tree-topping ceremony we would sing "Angels We Have Heard On High." This year Will said he wanted Jillian to have the honor of placing our heirloom angel on the tree.

When Christmas Eve arrived, our families gathered around for the simple ceremony. That's when Will handed Jillian the angel—with the engagement ring dangling from the angel's wrist. Jillian was speechless when Will got down on his knees to propose to her as both families looked on.

After we sang "Angels We Have Heard on High," Will and Jillian basked in congratulations from their families and proudly displayed her ring around the room. But as Jillian held our her hand to her grandmother Elizabeth, she let out a muffled cry. "Where did you get this ring?" she demanded of Will.

"It was my grandmother's," said Will, pointing to my mother.

"Would you mind taking it off, Jillian?" her grandmother asked. "I really must get a look at it!"

Everyone exchanged puzzled glances as Grandma Elizabeth held the ring up to the light. "I thought so," she exclaimed. "Look! My initials are intricately engraved inside this ring. Where did you find this? At an antique store?"

I glanced over at my mother, who was visibly shaken. "I've had it many years," she answered in a quavering voice.

"I don't believe I caught your last name, Margaret," said Jillian's grandmother.

When my mother couldn't seem to answer, I said, "It's Johnson."

"You must be joking!" Elizabeth exclaimed. "Was your husband by any chance named William Johnson?"

"Why, yes," I said, answering for my mother. "He was my father."

"There are lots of William Johnsons," my mother interjected. "It's a common name."

"Did your husband grow up in Indianapolis?" she asked.

"Why, yes!" I said. "Did you know him?"

"Did I know him? Your father and I were high school sweethearts. He proposed to me before he left for the war, and I accepted."

You could have heard a pin drop. Then Grandma Elizabeth, realizing there was nothing to do but explain, falteringly continued her story: "Bill was stationed in

Italy. We wrote one another for about three months, I was so young and fickle I—I found another—my husband, right here beside me. After the war, Bill's family left Indianapolis, so we never knew what happened."

"And you sent his ring back!" my mother suddenly said.

"Yes," Jillian's grandmother replied, "this is the same ring that I returned to Bill. Jillian's engagement ring is the ring I wore over fifty years ago!"

It was hard for any of us to grasp such a coincidence. No one in our family knew that my father had received a "Dear John" letter from his high school sweetheart when he was stationed in Italy during World War II. He'd met my mother in San Francisco after the war, where he'd taken a job. We never imagined there might have been any other woman in his life.

Suddenly it was clear why my mother had hidden that ring all those years. It was a painful reminder that she was not my father's first love. Now I was sure she regretted ever bringing that ring and her secret out of its hiding place.

Later that night when our guests had gone to bed, my mother and I were quietly doing the dishes together. I wanted to apologize for asking for the ring when suddenly she spoke. "All these years I've kept your father's first engagement a secret. I always felt like I was his second choice." I was about to protest when she held up her hand to stop me. "But God has given me the greatest Christmas gift of all tonight," she declared with a smile. "I finally came face to face with Elizabeth—the woman I envied my entire life!"

And then she began to chuckle. "All these years . . . all these years!" She kept repeating the phrase until gradually her chuckles grew into outright laughter—the first I'd heard from her since Dad's death three years before. Then she squealed, "She's not your father's type at all!"

From that night on, something softened inside my mother. In parting with the ring she'd kept hidden her whole adult life, she also parted with a fear that had kept her a prisoner. In its place she accepted the wonderful truth, one that her husband had known for years—his second choice had been the very best choice of his life.

A BABY BLANKET

WINONA SMITH

It was a spring Saturday, and though many activities clamored for my attention, I had chosen this time to sit and crochet, an activity I enjoyed but had once thought impossible.

Most of the time I don't mind being a "lefty"—I'm quite proud of it, actually. But I admit, it did cause me a few problems three years ago, when I wanted to help out with a project at church.

We were invited to crochet baby blankets, which would be donated to a local Crisis Pregnancy Center at Christmas. I wanted to participate but I knew nothing about how to crochet, and my left-handedness didn't help. I had trouble "thinking backwards."

I suppose where there is a will, there is a way, because a few of the ladies got together and taught me one stitch. That's all I needed. I learned that granny stitch, and before long I had a blanket made. I was so proud of my little accomplishment and it seemed, inexplicably, so important, that I made quite a few more that same year. I even included in each blanket, as a note of encouragement, a poem I had written that read:

Little girls are sweet in their ruffles all pink.

Little boys in overalls look divine.

But no matter which one that the Lord gives to you,

A better "Mom" He never could find.

All of a sudden, my thoughts were interrupted by the ringing of my telephone. I hurried to answer it, and to my surprise and delight, on the other end of the line was Karen Sharp, who had been one of my very best friends ever since elementary school. Karen, her husband Jim and their daughter Kim had moved away a few years ago. She was calling to say that she was in town for a couple of days and would like to come by. I was thrilled to hear her voice.

At last the doorbell rang. As I flung open the door, we both screamed, as if back in junior high. We hugged each other. Then questions began to fly. Finally, I guided Karen into the kitchen, where I poured a cool glass of tea for both of us and the conversation slowed.

To my delight, Karen seemed to be calm, rested and, most of all, self-assured, which were a few qualities that she had seemed to lose during the last few months before they moved away. I wondered what had caused the positive change.

As we talked and reminisced, Karen began to explain to me the true reasons for her family's move a few years ago. The original reason they had given me was that

Jim had a job offer in another city, which they could not afford to pass up. Even though it was Kim's senior year in high school, they still felt it necessary to make the move. Apparently, that had not been the biggest reason.

Karen reached into her purse and pulled out a photograph. When she handed it to me, I saw it was a beautiful little girl—maybe about two or three years old.

"This is my granddaughter, Kayla," Karen said.

I couldn't believe my ears. "You're a *grandmother*?" I asked. "I don't understand."

"You see," Karen went on, "Kim was a few months pregnant when we moved away. We had just found out, and Kim was having a really rough time dealing with it—she even talked about suicide. We were frantic. So we decided to move away, hoping that she would adjust more easily. When we finally settled in our new home, we hoped that Kim's outlook would begin to improve, but she became more and more depressed. No matter what we said, she felt worthless and like a failure. Then we found a woman named Mrs. Barber, a wonderful pregnancy counselor. She got Kim through some very rough times.

"As the time for delivery came closer, Kim still had not entirely made up her mind about whether to keep the baby or not. Her father and I prayed that she would. We felt prepared to give the baby a loving home—it was, after all, our first grandchild!

"Finally, the day came, and Kim had a six-pound, six-ounce baby girl. Mrs. Barber came to visit her in the hospital. She hugged Kim and told her how proud she was of her. Then she gave Kim a pastel-colored package containing a hand-crocheted baby blanket inside.

At this point, I felt a huge lump come into my throat, and I felt rather limp all over, but I tried not to show my feelings and kept listening to Karen's story.

Karen must have noticed the look on my face. She asked if I was all right. I assured her I was fine and asked her to please continue.

"As I said," she went on, "there was a baby blanket and a little personal note, something about little girls and their ruffles, little boys and their overalls, and a word of encouragement about becoming a new mom.

"We asked who made the blanket, and Mrs. Barber explained that some of the pregnancy centers have people who donate these blankets to new mothers and their babies. Her center was given the surplus from one of the other centers in the state, and she was glad to have one for Kim.

"Kim was so moved by the fact that a total stranger had thought enough to put so much time and effort into a blanket for her baby. She said it made her feel warm all over. She later told her dad and me that the little poem gave her a boost of confidence and helped her to make up her mind to keep little Kayla."

Karen's story had an even happier ending: A year later, Kim was married to a young man who loves both her and Kayla with all his heart. Karen grinned as she told me, then sobered. "My only regret is that I did not feel close enough to our friends here to have been able to lean on you all for support and comfort, instead of turning away.

"We are so thankful for so many things—especially the way everything turned out; but I think the one thing that we are the most thankful for is that kind person who made that little baby blanket for our daughter and her baby. I just wish I could give her a big hug and tell her how much she is loved and appreciated by our family."

I looked again at the photo of the sweet child in my hands. Then I leaned over to Karen and gave her a big hug.

THE RETURN OF THE BIBLE

CHARLES SWEITZER

When I entered the service during World War II, I was given a small pocket-size New Testament with my name inscribed on the inside front cover. Often I read passages for comfort from the stresses of Army life. But just before the invasion of Europe, we were told we weren't allowed to have any personal identification with us other than our dog tags. Reluctantly I handed in my Bible.

I made my way safely through Normandy, then moved with the American troops across France into Holland, Belgium and Germany. I often thought of my Bible, and when I prayed I could still remember God's promises written there.

At the war's end I returned to the States. Eventually I married and raised a family. One day in 1994 my daughter Nancy called me; she and her Danish husbands, Jorgen, had been unpacking after a recent move.

"One box was full of books," she said. "But I couldn't read a word of them because they were all written in Danish. So I asked Jorgen to look at them. He said they were hymnals he had bought ten years ago at an estate sale in Denmark.

"Jorgen sorted through the books, pulled out one and said, 'Here, this one's in

English.' You'll never guess what it was!" Nancy exclaimed. "On the inside cover was your name, Dad."

For fifty years I had been separated from my pocket-size Bible. To my delight it had come back to me.

A SWEATER COMES HOME

BECKY ALEXANDER

Late in World War II my father was on the battlefront in Germany. In March 1945, while his Canadian regiment awaited supplies, Dad was ordered to Aldershot, England, to be decorated by King George VI.

The weather was raw in Aldershot, but Dad had given away his regulation great-coat to a soldier back at the front. Shivering, he headed straight for the Red Cross center and picked from a bin full of sweaters a thick hand-knit one with a double collar. It fit perfectly under his tunic, warming him without breaking the uniform code.

After receiving the Military Medal for Bravery at Buckingham Palace, Dad rejoined the regiment and was issued another coat. He packed the sweater away in his kit.

Dad returned home safely to Canada in January 1946. His mother was glad to do his laundry again. While sorting his clothes, she held up the sweater, amazed. Then to my father's astonishment, she grabbed a pair of scissors and snipped the collar.

Like many women during the war, Grandma had knit sweaters for the young men overseas. She always put a note and postage money inside, so they could write back. "I prayed for the boys who would receive my handiwork, asking God to guide them safely home," she said. Many corresponded with her for years after.

While her hands had faithfully knitted, other Hands had guided her son safely home. Inside the collar of the sweater was some postage money—and a note she had written to a boy overseas.

THE PRAYER

SUSAN WALES

As a single woman, I was always the person my friends called on when they needed a baby-sitter, a ride to the airport, or a shoulder to cry on. Someone would always suggest, "Call Susan. She's not married. She can do it."

Many of my friends would admonish me to set boundaries. "You have to earn a living," they'd tell me. Still, my parents had taught me to help others, so if I was available, I'd give a helping hand or a listening ear.

One particularly hectic morning my office phone rang. It was Ann Perdue, a good friend, calling from California, where she was on a business trip. She sounded troubled. I was immediately concerned, but as I glanced nervously at my watch, my friends' advice echoed: *You have to earn a living; tell her you'll call back.* I argued with myself, *I'll run behind with my appointments for the rest of the day.* Finally I stifled a heavy sigh, pushed back a stack of papers, and asked Ann what the problem was.

Ann said a business acquaintance of hers had just been rushed into emergency surgery. Doctors had found a tumor in his neck that appeared to be malignant. "The surgeon told him there's a risk his vocal cords will be severed in surgery," she explained. "This man is a dynamic speaker who addresses thousands of young people each year about his faith, and he may never speak again!"

"I'm so sorry, Ann" I said. "Is there anything I can do?"

"Would you pray for him with me, Susan? I don't know a soul in California, and I knew I could call you."

I nervously glanced at my appointment book. It was crammed. People were backed up in the lobby waiting for me. But how could I tell Ann no?

"Sure," I said. "Let's pray right now."

As Ann and I prayed over the phone, we sensed God's power at work. By the time we hung up, I felt confident this man's surgery would be a success. Then it suddenly occurred to me I didn't even know his name."

Years passed. Spring found me busy as always—this time getting ready for my own wedding. Ann called to congratulate me, and out of the blue she asked, "Do you remember the man we prayed for on the phone several years ago? The one who needed throat surgery?"

"Sure," I replied. "I always wondered what happened to him. How is he?"

Ann giggled. "Why don't you tell me? You're marrying him!"

For a moment I couldn't speak. I had no idea my fiancé was the man Ann and I had prayed for that morning. Even though Ken had told me about his throat surgery and the miraculous recovery, I had never made the connection.

"Ann!" I finally blurted. "Isn't it amazing? God allowed me to pray for my future husband—and answered my prayer—when Ken was a total stranger to me!"

That day I realized the real business of life is people. What you give away to others—time, prayer, a listening ear—will come back to you somehow. And it just might be as love.

WHEN WE ASK

JOAN WESTER ANDERSON

What goes around comes around ... Roberta Eschenbaum, a farmwife living outside Miller, South Dakota, certainly knows this to be true. She had taken a quick trip into Miller one morning and rushed home to get the noon meal on the table for the men. As she drove, she was also keeping an eye out for her father, who lived alone and had emphysema. "He didn't drive much except for the twelve miles out to our farm," she says, "so I always knew that if he needed help on the road, someone would stop." But it was still a worry for her, and she often prayed for his safety.

There was no sign of Roberta's father's car. Instead, up ahead, she saw another vehicle stopped at the side of the road, a man peering into the engine. "I was in a hurry, and although I always help people I know, this man was a stranger," Roberta says. She should have kept going. But something told her to stop, and she did.

The driver was having trouble with his battery, so Roberta drove to a neighboring farm, borrowed booster cables, drove back, and got the car going. "This is wonderful." The driver thanked her and reached for his wallet. "Could I ...?"

"No payment necessary." Roberta smiled, getting back in her car. "Just return this favor by helping the next person you find stalled along a road."

"I certainly will!" The man waved as she pulled out.

Two weeks later, Roberta's father phoned, with an interesting story to tell. "I went to an auction about fifty miles southwest of here—" he began.

"Fifty miles!" Roberta was aghast. "Dad, you never drive that far alone!"

"—and I got a flat tire on the way home."

By now Roberta was in a panic. The area he was describing was a backcountry road, with little or no chance of anyone coming by. Nor could her father have changed his own tire, weakened as he was. "What happened?" she asked.

"You wouldn't believe it. A nice motorist came along right away and changed my tire. But when I offered to pay him, he said no. Seems a woman outside of Miller had given him a battery jump two weeks ago, and told him to pass on the favor. He was paying a debt to her."

Roberta felt love surrounding her like a hug. "I think God knew Dad was going to do that, and so He arranged a rescue ahead of time," she says. "I look for evidence of His presence all the time—and I always find it."

GRANDMA'S BIBLE

CHERYL DEEP

I stared at our seven-month-old baby girl, Chelsea, in the hospital crib. As I tucked up her blanket, my eyes rested on the old Dillon family Bible I kept in the crib with her. It had belonged to my grandmother, who died when I was thirteen. I cherished that Bible as I had cherished my grandmother. She always soothed my childhood hurts and fears; to this day I still miss her. The Bible had rested in her hands during her funeral service. My mother removed it just before the coffin lid was lowered and later gave it to me.

But even Grandmother probably could not have soothed the hurt and fear my husband Lance and I now faced. Earlier that day the specialists at University Medical Center in Tucson had finally diagnosed the baffling condition that was slowly but surely draining the life from our first child.

"Chelsea has an extremely rare birth defect called severe combined immunodeficiency syndrome," our doctor informed us. "SCIDS interferes with the normal functioning of her immune system. She has virtually no natural defenses against infection. Her bone marrow doesn't produce the necessary cells."

I stood statue-still and stared at him. I remembered the movie *The Boy in the Plastic Bubble* about a child with the same condition. All along we'd hoped it was some obscure but defeatable bug causing the fever, diarrhea and weight loss that ravaged Chelsea. I had prayed that somewhere in the mighty arsenal of modern medicine was the right drug, the magic bullet that would cure her. The immunologist carefully explained that the only option was a bone marrow transplant—a risky procedure that at best had about a fifty percent chance of success.

The only option.

We needed to transfer her to a hospital that did this sort of operation as soon as possible, he had said. There were only a few in the entire country.

Now as I stood over Chelsea's crib I smoothed the blanket and pushed the old Bible off to the side. Its leather cover was worn soft with use. As my child slept I closed my eyes and hoped for a miracle.

The next day we decided on Memorial Sloan-Kettering in Manhattan for the procedure because of their slightly-higher-than-average success rate. But now came the enormous problem of transporting Chelsea from Tucson to New York without exposing her to many people. Chelsea couldn't afford to catch even a cold. Any worsening in her condition would delay surgery. A simple flu bug could kill her.

Driving there was out of the question. She couldn't be off her IV fluids for that long. Commercial airliners posed too much hazard of contracting contagious disease, and big airports were even worse. We needed a private plane, but Chelsea's condition was not considered acutely critical—a criterion that had to be met before our insurance company would agree to cover the enormous cost of a jet. The catch-22 was that if Chelsea did become that critical, she would probably be too sick to have the surgery.

Lance and I were at wit's end. We didn't sleep, we barely ate. There had to be something we could do. We made countless phone calls. Finally we heard about a group called Corporate Angels, which provides free flights for sick children aboard private planes. The flights conduct normal business travel, and patients hitch along. Corporate Angels found us a flight leaving that Friday out of Denver bound nonstop for New York. A miracle was in our grasp.

"Dear God," I prayed, "now please help up get to Denver. I know You have Your ways. We'll just keep on trying."

Denver was too far to drive. We got the number of a private medevac company. Maybe we could pay for the flight ourselves. But when I talked to Judy Barrie, a paramedic whose husband Jim piloted the medevac plane, she gave me the bad news. "The flight will cost six thousand dollars, minimum," she said. We didn't have six thousand dollars. Our finances had been stretched to the limit.

I thanked Judy and said good-bye. "Wait," she said suddenly as I was about to hang up. "I really want to help you. I'm not promising anything, but I'll talk to Jim. Maybe he can figure this out."

When I hung up I had the strangest feeling that these people would be able to do something about what was increasingly a hopeless situation. An hour later Jim Barrie called back. "Listen, I've got a friend flying back an empty plane from Phoenix to Denver in the morning," Jim told me. "If you can get to the field by six-thirty, you can hitch along."

Perfect. Chelsea could handle the drive to Phoenix. But I was almost afraid to ask the next question. "Jim, what will it cost?"

"Cost? Heck, not a thing. This guy's a friend, and he's got to get his plane up anyway."

I was faint with relief. These total strangers had taken a huge step in saving the life of my child. I didn't know what to say. The word thanks didn't seem big enough.

You could do us one little favor, though," Jim added. "Judy and I would like to meet Chelsea."

Chelsea was awake and even a bit playful when Jim and Judy arrived at the hospital. While Jim talked to Lance about finding our way around the Phoenix airport, Judy and I chatted. Her eyes kept flitting over to the crib. Then I noticed she was staring at Grandma's Bible. One time when Judy was leaning over Chelsea, her fingers brushed it. Finally, as they were about to go, Judy asked, "Where are you from?" I told her Pittsburgh.

"I'm from Pittsburgh too," she said slowly. "Well, the suburb Carnegie actually."

"My mother is from Carnegie," I said. I felt a shiver go through me. "Virginia Everett. Dillon was her maiden name."

"Virginia Dillon?" Judy said, eyes wide. "My father was Howard Dillon."

"Uncle Howard?" I was stunned.

Judy nodded. It was as if a current of electricity had jumped between us. Now I could see why her face had seemed faintly familiar. Judy Barrie was my cousin Judy Dillon. "I haven't seen you since . . . ," I started to say. Judy's eyes jumped again to the Bible.

"Since Grandma's funeral twenty years ago," she finished the sentence. "That's the Bible she was holding."

We fell into each other's arms. I knew then that all would be well with Chelsea. The odds against this crossing of paths were simply too great. This was meant to be.

Chelsea got her bone marrow transplant and four months later she left the hospital with a healthy immune system. She is, as they say, a medical miracle.

And then there was that other miracle. I like to think of it as my grandmother's miracle. In a sense, even twenty years after her funeral, she was reaching out to comfort me and to assure me that with God all things are possible.

(continued from page vi)

www.guidepostsbooks.com
Series Editor: Patricia S. Klein
Designed by Monica Elias
Jacket photo courtesy of Photodisc
Typeset by Composition Technologies, Inc.
Typists: Rachel Eden and Judith Silvio
Printed in the United States of America

This original Guideposts Book was created by the Book and Inspirational Media Division of the company that publishes *Guideposts*, a monthly magazine filled with true stories of hope and inspiration.

Guideposts is available by subscription. All you have to do is write to Guideposts, 39 Seminary Hill Road, Carmel, New York 10512. When you subscribe, each month you can count on receiving exciting new evidence of God's presence, His guidance and His limitless love for all of us.

Guideposts Books are available on the World Wide Web at www.guidepostsbooks.com. Follow our popular book of devotionals, *Daily Guideposts*, and read excerpts from some of our best-selling books. You can also send prayer requests to our Monday morning Prayer Fellowship and read stories from recent issues of our magazines, *Guideposts, Angels on Earth*, and *Guideposts for Teens.*